Finding Foxholes

Also by Faye Berger

Gumption, Lessons on Old Age, Loneliness, and a Hotdish

Finding Foxholes

A World War II Infantry Route,
Then . . . and 48 Years Later

Faye Berger with Russel Albrecht

North Star Press of St. Cloud, Inc.
St. Cloud, Minnesota

Dedicated to our World War II Veterans.

First Edition: March 2014

Printed in the United States of America

Published by
North Star Press of St. Cloud, Inc.
P.O. 451
St. Cloud, Minnesota 56302

northstarpress.com

Table of Contents

BATTLE ROUTE OF THE
120TH INFANTRY REGIMENT 1944

(History of the 120th Infantry Regiment)

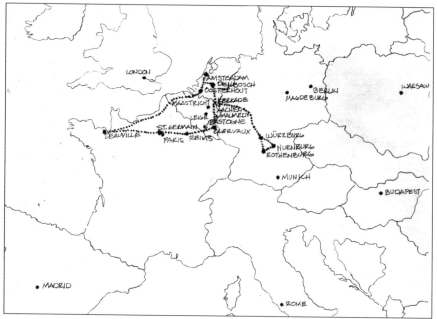

1992 Route of Road Trip (Author's Collection)

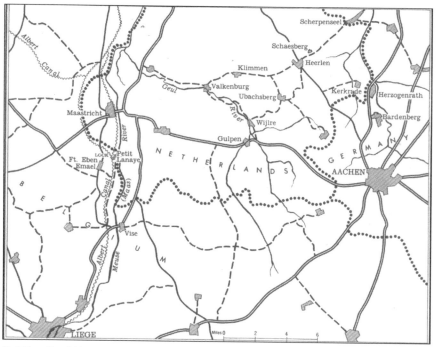

Fort Eben Email-Maastricht- Kerkrade (History of the 120th Infantry Regiment)

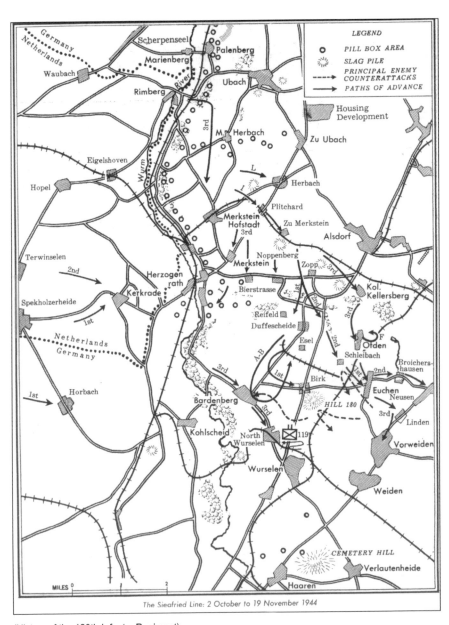

(History of the 120th Infantry Regiment)

Foreword

L ITTLE DID I KNOW THAT A TRIP in 1992 would offer the framework for *Finding Foxholes*, now twenty-two years later. Certainly, had I known, I would have taken better notes. The trip was with my husband and my dad as we traveled across Europe to retrace Dad's World War II infantry route. As it was, the car trip offered the perfect opportunity to audio-tape my dad's stories of his combat experience.

Long known for his vivid and compelling storytelling, Private First Class Russel E. Albrecht from the small town of Morgan, Minnesota, brings to light the basic realities of war on the front lines: the hardships, the victories, the bonding of comrades, the duty to country, the sheer determination to stay alive. *This* is history first-hand.

The travelogue framework then gives a stage for Private Albrecht's stories, filling in with historical backdrop plus modern-day dynamics of baby boomer and aging parent. A third dimension, the tidbits of 1940 through 1945 history preceding each of Private Albrecht's accounts, draws the reader back to the war years.

Private First Class Russel E. Albrecht served in the Infantry of the U.S. Army, Thirtieth Division, 120th Regiment from March 27, 1944, to November 28, 1945. As a "replacement," he landed at Omaha Beach, fought at the Siegfried line, the Ardennes, the Battle of the Bulge, crossing of the Rhine, then on to the German autobahn. He was wounded twice and was hospitalized for pneumonia, bronchitis, and pleurisy. A Bronze Star was awarded to him for calling artillery fire upon his own position. This first-hand account of a combat rifleman brings to solid ground the base nature of war.

My dad has been gone more than ten years now, but his stories are as alive as ever, and I am privileged to share them. But what might Russ Albrecht want out of all this? It's simple really: a renewal of patriotism. He might point a finger and tell us that, despite all of our country's troubles, we still live in the best place on earth. "Be thankful," he'd say. "We have freedom and opportunity. Fly the flag with honor." He also might lecture on the value of hard work. "Just buckle down and tend to your knittin'. That's how things get done." I can see him saying that.

Although this is only one soldier's story, my hope is that it might spark countless stories—from all of our vets from all of our wars. We as a thankful country must always remember and honor our veterans, but also we need to hear their stories so that we can learn. And the stories we need to hear first—the stories that are fast fading—are those from our most senior veterans, the veterans of World War II.

The Travelers

SOMETIMES A SEARCH for old memories can turn up something even better. Better as in extraordinary, or unique, even off-the-map coincidental. What if you ask yourself out of the blue, "How did *this* happen?" Well, that was what was in store for us—my dad, my husband, and me—when we set off on our trip across Europe in 1992. Searching for World War II remembrances set us up in a big way for lessons and a very special find.

The trip came about as one of those light-bulb ideas that surfaced at just the right time in my life. Likely, I got the idea from one of those motivational speakers, who have always grabbed my attention, the ones who push you to achieve your goals. But what I'm not sure about is the subject matter: war. Why was *I* the one in my family to have this heavy interest? After all, I was a girl, and I didn't even come along until after Dad came home—a baby boomer born in 1947.

It was just Mom and my two older sisters, Diane and Mary Jane, who were only three and four years old, who waved goodbye to Dad. That was the spring of 1944. They were the ones carrying on life in the little town of Morgan, Minnesota, while he was gone those two years, waiting for his letters, saying their prayers for his safe return. My younger sister, Deb, came along much later in 1956, more than a decade after the war. With a spread of seventeen years among us girls, Deb was definitely the baby and definitely set apart from those war years.

Dad and Mom with my older sisters, Mary Jane and Diane. (Author's collection)

For me, being in this middle category of siblings and spaced quite a distance either way, I spent several years like an only child. Some might think of it as lonely, but I thought it was more of a privilege. I had a bedroom all to myself. I also had a certain amount of autonomy what with Mom and Dad preoccupied with Mary Jane and Diane as teenagers and Deb as an infant. I busied myself with the usual paper dolls and coloring books, and if my dad was available, I tagged after him when he explored the woods or when he went fishing—I thought he deserved a boy. I thought I was the one to fill in.

But I also spent a good deal of time imagining the dark and scary consequences of war. Those were the fifties when bomb shelter drills were common in schools, and we worried about the Cold War. I remember a particular fear at the sound of an airplane flying over our little town, and if I happened to be walking home from school with a plane high overhead, I would break into a run. But I knew a lot about the war too because of my dad's particular gift for telling stories, and the stories he told most often were of his two-year duty in Europe in the infantry.

Private First Class Russel E. Albrecht landed at Omaha Beach and fought across France and Belgium, through the Battle of the Bulge and the crossing of the Rhine. That's a lot of world travel for a small-town, family man in rural Minnesota back in the forties. And that's how he looked at it too—a chance to see beyond the tragedy of war. Well, first he had to survive it, but that's one of his stories.

So the stories were with me from early childhood on, and as an adult, I sought out books and movies about World War II, especially those about the fighting in Europe. Even songs from that era—Glenn Miller and the big bands—have always been sentimental for me. And up until Dad's last days, I continued to prompt him for retelling the stories I practically knew by heart.

The fact that Russ Albrecht was a storyteller might say something about his ability to ride out the bumps in life. He could transform misfortune into a lesson on life—always a good story, most would agree. One can only assume that this ability even helped him get through a war. Curious and with an amazing eye for detail, he observed and learned, was quick, and made friends easily. He was a positive guy.

Russ loved the small farming community of Morgan, Minnesota. He always boasted that Morgan had the best tasting water and that soldiers from the Midwest, especially Minnesota, were the healthiest in the nation. My sisters and I all took this to heart.

After the war, Russ had aspirations to study the growing technology of air conditioning, one of the programs offered to veterans by Uncle Sam. But another long stint away from home just didn't have an appeal. Instead, he set upon the task of rebuilding his life by resuming work with his father at the family grocery store, and when his father died in the fifties, Russ continued on with the store for another twenty years. That's when the grocery chain forced him out of business because sales didn't justify a truck delivery to little Morgan. One of those bumps in life. But the very day the store sold, Russ was offered a job as bookkeeper at the local gas station. That job he maintained for another twenty-five years. He retired at age eighty-eight.

Russ and Lorraine raised four daughters, like I said, two were born before the war and two afterwards. As the daughters one by one married and the family expanded, Russ liked to boast that theirs was the ideal family: all healthy, all accounted for. But that would abruptly change. In the space of only thirteen months in the mid-eighties, Russ lost his oldest daughter, a son-in-law, and then Lorraine, his wife and partner of forty-eight years. The suddenness and the enormity of these losses had their effect on Russ: he didn't sleep well, and he became quiet.

Our trip to Europe sprouted from the time in Russ's life when he was living alone. True to his resilient nature, in due time he became engaged again in life. He melded into this new role of self-sufficiency and new friendships, in fact some very unlikely friendships. He was back to being his old self. Back to telling stories. Certainly, he didn't *need* this trip, but as it turned out, *I* did.

Sure, my husband and I loved the idea of a history hunt and the pure adventure of foreign travel. That was our model for a good trip. And we both were fascinated with Dad's stories. Wilt, though not a veteran himself—too young for Korea and too old for Vietnam—was always engaged in Dad's stories as if he were an integral part of them, always piecing those stories together with memories he had as a young boy during World War II growing up in Winona, Minnesota. And with an architectural background to boot, Wilt naturally was eager to observe European historical sites. The travel dynamics were there, and they were thrilling.

But privately, I needed something deeper. As the middle daughter who bonded with Dad all of those years growing up, I wanted to make up for times when, as an adult, I was absent or when I caused him worry, when my busy life got in the way of remembering. I needed to give him a gift so special, so perfect, that he would know my admiration once and for all. High expectations, you might say.

Russel Albrecht as a young boy during World War I when his brother and sister were serving in the war. (Author's collection)

As you probably have guessed, Russ Albrecht didn't operate on emotions, none of that gut-feeling, intuitive nuance that drives *my* decisions—no, he faced situations squarely based on his values, period. At age thirty-four, he was one of the oldest U.S. infantrymen on the Western Front, and he just might have been the smallest too, measuring in at five-foot-five and 119 pounds. You could worry, certainly, that these are not optimum physical attributes for the demand and rigors of a foot soldier on the front line of battle. One officer in fact noted off the cuff "cannon fodder" when he looked at Albrecht and another one of the older replacements. But Russ's age and size seemed to work as a benefit with his clear thinking and cunning agility. And, as I said, Russ had an advantage: a positive approach to life. Inspired by a brother and sister who served in World War I, Russ *wanted* to be part of the war effort after Pearl Harbor. A true patriot, he didn't question serving for his country. He *wanted* to serve.

But Russ Albrecht didn't take life for granted. When faced with his new destiny, he decided to rely on a Bible verse, which he claimed made all the difference. It's the one that says pray for something, believe in it, and you will receive it.[1] To a man not overly religious, and even critical of the church at times, those matter-of-fact words at that critical time in his life made a lot of sense.

Then for added good measure, Russ carried with him two crayon-colored pages from his little girls. Neatly folded to fit his shirt pocket and wrapped in cellophane, those pages survived combat battle, too. He carried them at all times there next to his heart. Today my sister Diane has both of them proudly displayed in her home. Dad insisted that the two always stay together.

I never saw my dad cry. But I did see his hand tremble at a parade when he saluted the U.S. flag. From the curb where we sat, he jumped to attention at the first sight of the Color Guard, and he held that salute until the band had passed. When I think back, even the clothes he wore most often spoke from his heart—plaids of red, white, and blue were his favorites, always with the tag "MADE IN THE U.S.A."

1944 – The two colored pages carried by Private Albrecht. (Author's Collection)

[1]Mark 11:24

The Trip

THE NOTION OF SOMEHOW GETTING DAD back to Europe seemed like a fantasy, but in my mid-forties with grown children and suddenly with more freedom to travel, I zeroed in on the opportunity. "What about a trip to Europe with Dad to retrace his infantry route?" I cautiously asked Wilt when considering travel options for the next year. Another trip possibility for us at the time was an opportunity to work at a Mexican mission that particularly appealed to Wilt as an architect and that we had agreed would be the perfect cross-cultural experience for us. I put that thought on hold. "Dad isn't getting any younger . . . seems like this might be the right time . . . we can do the mission thing next year . . . what do you think?" I blurted. I worried that even though Wilt respected Dad to the utmost and thoroughly enjoyed his company, he might hesitate on around-the-clock Russ Albrecht for a couple of weeks. That would be reasonable for any son-in-law, I thought. As a matter of fact, that would be reasonable for a daughter, too. But Wilt jumped at the idea like he was thinking about it himself. "Yes! Let's do it!" he said, eyes wide with excitement. "I've got a map of Europe around here somewhere. Let's check it out."

From that minute on, we were in trip mode. Planning started with a quick review of Dad's stories and a vague tracking of them on the map—crossing the Atlantic on the *Queen Mary*, landing at Omaha Beach, fighting on the front lines in Belgium, the Netherlands, and Germany—including the Battle of the Bulge, hospitalization in Paris, crossing the Rhine, post-war duty in Germany, and waiting for orders in Reims. That was a lot of territory to cover in ten days.

Ten was the magic number we agreed upon when phoning Dad with the idea—certainly more than just a week for such a distance with so many destinations, but certainly nothing extravagant for us, all leaning to conservative spending, as we were. We had jobs after all, even Dad. Though retired, he was supplementing his Social Security with that part-time job as bookkeeper at the local gas station. True to his Midwestern values, he insisted on paying his share of the trip. Respectful of that, we agreed, knowing that, with Dad's more limited budget, we would plan for modest accommodations. Youth hostels? That could work, we thought. Cheap airfare? The best deal extended only through mid-March which, of course, most travelers would know is not the optimal travel time for Europe given its northern latitude. "But, what's so bad about cool weather," we reasoned, considering our budgets again. "March is close enough to spring." Naïvely, we hoped the tulips might be in bloom.

The task was to map our route, staying as much on course as possible with Dad's actual experience. We would rent a car, economy of course, and have the ability to stop whenever and wherever we wanted—a custom-made tour across Europe. Wilt was more than happy to drive, a settling thought for me because he is Mr. Calm at the wheel. I would be the navigator.

The challenge would be to schedule reasonable hours on the road given the compressed itinerary and given the age of our travel companion. For eighty-two years of age, Dad was in very good health and always had been, but everyone knows travel can be demanding. Some might say that taking an eighty-two-year-old on a road trip even here at home, let alone in a foreign country, might be asking for trouble. And what exactly is the value of a once-of-a-lifetime trip if that senior gets seriously sick or injured? It could turn quickly into a *last*-of-a-lifetime trip. So we thought it through and agreed: easy does it. We would monitor our energy levels on the go.

When finally the basic plan seemed doable, we knuckled down to research the countries, the cities, and then the fine details of actual military routes. Big note here: This was 1990, *before* the phenomenon of Google and Mapquest, which meant, instead of a few hours on a computer, we spent long hours in map stores and libraries. It also meant we missed out on a lot of particulars and rich history so easily accessible now on our computers. Dad, for his research contribution, dug out from his stash of war mementos a remarkably detailed account of his regiment, *History of the 120th Infantry Regiment*.

The most important detail we considered only at the last minute. "What about bringing along my office recorder and a few diskette tapes for recording Russ's stories?" Wilt asked. "Won't take up much room, and we'll have plenty of time in the car going from place to place. We *need* to get his stories on tape. What do you think?"

Of course, why didn't we think of that before? The idea was brilliant. We gathered the recording supplies, along with plenty of extra batteries. *Now,* we were armed and ready for our journey into history.

Ready, that is to say, except for last minute anxiety about family dynamics. When my older sister called to ask if she might accompany us, I had to hold true to our plan. With such a large agenda and such a small car, another passenger didn't seem practical. If she came along, I would want my younger sister along too—a family thing. You see the dilemma. All I could do was promise that something else would come up for all of us girls. And it did.

Meanwhile, Russ Albrecht was packing his bag, which, of course, included his plaid red, white and blue shirts, his navy sweater, and his blue-and-white cap. All aboard!

1992 – Travel journal. (Author's Collection)

***

December 9, 1941: Radio address by President Roosevelt—". . . The course that Japan has followed for the past ten years in Asia has paralleled the course of Hitler and Mussolini in Europe and Africa. Today, it has become far more than a parallel. It is collaboration so well calculated that all the continents of the world, and all the oceans, are now considered by the Axis strategists as one gigantic battlefield . . ."

77th Congress, 1st session, Doc. No. 148, U.S. Declarations of War, www.ibiblio.org.

Private Albrecht:
CALL TO DUTY

Before the Japs hit us, like in 1940, most people then thought, "Just stay out of there. We got no doggone business over there." That was the main topic. "What do you want over there?" you know. "Old Adolf has got problems over there—why not let them settle their problems." That was the general opinion. There were even several fellows that I know thought Hitler was really doing a pretty good job for Germany. And, I guess as far as for the people's concern, he was. But, they didn't know what all was going on. That was the whole problem.

Then once, of course, the Japs hit Pearl Harbor, well, that was a different story altogether. Then everybody buckled down and got into it. It sure made you think, you know, when you had a family and you wanted to be part of the war effort. You didn't want to be left out, but you didn't want to leave your family either.

Like me, well everybody said . . . in fact I remember my sister-in-law said, "Well, what the heck you worried about? You aren't going to have to go, for heaven's sake. You're married, and you've got two kids." Even when I finished basic, she said, "Now where you think you're going to go? Oh, for heaven's sake, what's the matter with you? Why in the world are you scaring your wife that way? You shouldn't even talk about that. You know better than that. At your age you aren't going up in the Front Line."

I argued with her and it didn't do much good, but that's exactly where I went. So that was it.

Finding Foxholes

***

1942-1945 : "For a new recruit, military service began with a physical examination, often indifferently done by a local doctor working under contract. After a couple of weeks to get his civilian affairs in order, the recruit would be on his way by bus or train to Fort Snelling . . . Arriving at the fort, recruits were marched to barracks and put to work with mop and broom . . . A thorough army physical followed the next day, as did the all-important Army General Qualification Test."
Minnesota Historical Society, *Fort Snelling's Last War*, 2009, www.mnhs.org

Private Albrecht:
THE PHYSICAL

A whole busload from Redwood County went down to Fort Snelling for physicals. The process was you had your physical and then you went home until you were called, then you went down to Fort Snelling again. You waited until they assigned you to whatever camp you were going to head for.

My physical was routine except at the heart doctor. When I got there they took me out of the line, and I couldn't figure what the heck was the matter. I didn't know anything was wrong. Then I went in a room with a couple of specialists, and they checked it all over and made me go through a bunch of exercises and said that I had to go over to the hospital. So they kept me there seven days at Fort Snelling, and all the rest of them went home in the bus that night.

Then on the seventh day they said I should go over to the hospital and pick up some x-rays. So I went over. It was a nice day, and on the way back walking over to the VA Center, I sat on a bench. I saw that the envelope wasn't sealed so I took the x-rays out to look at them. The papers said the heart was normal but the tubes or whatever it is going to the heart or from the heart, I forget which way it was, were oversized, and that's what made my heart work so much faster.

So I took that over to the doctors and they looked it over and they made me go through some exercise and they both shook their heads and put a big red "X" across my paper. They said, "You go out that last door over there, that's the final doctor, just give him the stuff."

So I did—I handed him the papers and he said, "Okay, you can go." He was a Jewish looking fellow. I got as far as the door, and, "Hey, wait a minute," he said. *"Wait a minute. What's that name . . . Albrecchhttt?"*—he brought it out real German.

I said, "I never heard it pronounced that way, it's 'Albright [phon.].'"

He looked at a boy there sitting at his desk, a young guy, and he says, "Hey, you like to erase?"

"Yah."

"Well, erase that red 'X' on there if you can. I think we can use this guy."

And that was it. So, then I went home, and first thing Doc Johnson saw me and said, "Hey, what the Sam Hill they keep you for?"

I explained it to him, and he said, "Now tomorrow morning when you get up, don't smoke, don't take a drink of water or anything else, don't exercise, just get out of bed and come down to the office."

I said, "I'll be down there, but what the heck's going on?"

"Well," he said, "don't worry about it. It isn't costing you anything—I just want to find out something."

"Okay." So I did that—I went down and had to lay down there, and he hooked me up like a TV and took some tests, breathing oxygen and got that all done. He looked it all over and he said, "Well, Russ, there is certainly a place in the Army for you. There is no doubt that you can get in supply or something like that. But," he said, "no infantry or heavy artillery." He said, "I wouldn't be responsible for sending you on a hike with a pack on your back."

Well, I didn't know what to think, but that's what it was. So I told him, "I have an idea, Doc, when I get down there, they aren't going to say, 'Well, Mr. Albrecht, what would you like to be in?'"

So I was a few days at home and then pretty soon the call came for infantry, and down to Camp Wolters, Texas, I went—took the basics, sixteen weeks of basic down there. It was supposed to be a very, very rough camp, a hard camp, strict training, and I am sure it was. Whenever we would have a checkup there, every so often you would have to run through the line and get checked, and when I would get to the heart doctor, out I would go. Or they would be rechecking and when we finished basic, then you took your test for overseas duty. When I got to the heart doctor: "Out you come!"

Just then our captain came by, Captain Kennedy, and he said, "What's the matter with Albrecht?"

"Well, I don't know, the heart—we got to check that more."

The captain said, "Oh, hell, he's a good man."

Well, okay, then in I went. So that was it. From there on, there were no more tests. That was it. But of all the times they asked for blood in Camp Walters there in training or even overseas or whenever they needed blood, they would never take mine. They said, "Your heart is working enough the way it is without taking any blood."

But I went through the whole thing—a twenty-five-mile hike with a full field pack on my back, and I had a big guy next to me about one and again the size of me, and I carried his rifle the last two miles of the hike so he could make it. So there you are.

1944 – Private Russel E. Albrecht. (Author's Collection)

Faye Berger with Russel Albrecht

***

1942: The popular Fred Waring & His Pennsylvanians performed "America Calling" composed by Meredith Wilson, released in 1942, Syracuse University Library, WWII Songs, http://library.syr.edu

Private Albrecht:
THE VERSE

When you are about that age and you're going into a war, well, you know it isn't the Fourth of July celebration—chances are that a lot of you going in aren't going to come back. So, it makes you think, whether you like it or not.

We got a little Testament given to us from church—that's before I went in, just before I went in. I was reading in that one day, and I ran across this passage that said, "Pray for something, believe you will receive it, and you will." For some reason or other that kind of stuck in my head, and I kept thinking, well, in other words, whatever you pray for and you believe that you're going to get it, you will get it.

Well, then you can stop and think, Well, my gosh, you know, I could pray that I wasn't going to go in the Army, or I could pray that I'd be 4F, or that if I get in, I could be in service supply or something like that right here in the United States. *But that didn't sound reasonable. Who am I to ask for something like that? Finally, I came up with the idea that in my prayers I would put in that I would go in for whatever they want me for and go wherever they want, and no matter where I went or what I was in, I'd come home on my own power whenever the thing is over. And that my wife and two kids would be waiting for me when I come home. They'd be there. Nothing was going to happen to them.*

And so from then on, that was my prayer. That even was the reason, I suppose, for a lot of the way I acted. I figured, well okay, if I'm going to believe in that, if I want that to really happen, I can't go messing around all over the place and doing what's wrong. I'm going to have to watch myself and see that I'm on the straight and narrow path there all the way through because if I want that to happen, I have got to be right on my side. So, that's the way I figured all the way through. I wasn't going to get messed up with anybody or anything like that and that was it, period. Once I got started on that, there was nobody who could change my mind. I don't care what happened, I would be coming home.

13

***

1941: "The USO [United Service Organization] was founded in 1941 in response to a request from President Franklin D. Roosevelt to provide morale and recreation services to U.S. uniformed military personnel. Roosevelt was elected as its honorary chairman. This request brought together six civilian organizations: the Salvation Army, Young Men's Christian Association (YMCA), Young Women's Christian Association (YWCA), National Catholic Community Services, National Travelers Aid Association and the National Jewish Welfare Board."

"History of the USO," www.usonyc.org

Private Albrecht:
THE TWELVE-HOUR PASS

After Basic, we got what they called a "delay in route"—you had ten days. So I came scooting home, and it took awhile on some of them slow trains. But then I had to get to Maryland within them ten days, and I did. Went down to Minneapolis and got on the Zephyr going from Minneapolis to Chicago and then on another big train, the Ann Rutledge, and got into Maryland, at Fort Meade. We were there for, oh, I'd say a week.

The camp was kind of in a ravine there, and you had, oh, like tarpaper shacks. That's where we stayed until we were assigned to whatever boat we were going on. There was a hurricane along the East Coast. We knew it was darn windy, but we were down in that ravine, so we didn't get too much of it.

You could get a pass from six in the morning until six in the evening, or you could get a pass from six in the evening until six in the morning—a twelve-hour pass. I went with another guy—we took both of them—one of 'em to Washington, D.C., and then the next time we went, we took the opposite one to New York City because New York City never closed up, always open.

In Washington, D.C., we went to the Smithsonian Institute and all that and over by the White House. There, well, we had to keep moving. You couldn't stop even along the fence, but I saw Eleanor with the dog out there on the lawn. The minute you stopped to look through the fence, somebody would say, "Come on, move on, move on."

Now, New York—I always figured you know as long as the old government wanted me in there and they're paying the bill, I'm going to see every damn

1944 – Postcard "times Square, the heart of New York's hotel and theater district and the playground of the nation. This postcard was purchased atop the Empire State Building, N.Y.C." (Author's Collection)

thing I can. I had a buddy in the camp there at Meade, and he had ideas like mine. There was another fella who wanted to go along with us, but he was quite a drinker and would go and get all tanked up. I told him, "I don't think you would care much for it because we're not stopping for any drinks."

He said, "Well, what's wrong with stopping for a drink?"

"Well," I said, "not a thing, but you can do that any time. You don't want to do that when you're going to see something. I'm going into New York. I've never been there. I want to see what the heck it's all about."

He thought it over, and he decided he'd like to come along with us. So, I said, "Well, that's fine but just remember that." So he did.

We got on a bus. I don't remember what street we had to get off to go down on the subway and get in the subway train. We didn't know beans from buckshot, but it seems you get where you're going. I knew Forty-Second and Broadway and Forty-Second Street from some movie or something, so when we got to that, well, I said, "That's where we get out." But first I noticed on the map that the subway went to Grand Central Station, and that's where I wanted to go first. Of course, both guys said, "Well, what the heck. Why do we want another train station?"

I said, "Don't worry about it. That's where we're going to go."

So we did, and we got there—heck of a big station—and I told them to wait by the one door there, and I was going to find something.

I found what I was looking for—I didn't know that much but somebody had told me about it. I found the USO desk, or whatever it was, and the gal said, "Can I help you?"

"Ya," I said, "I want to look over New York City. We're on a pass for twelve hours."

She said, "Where would you like to go?"

Well, the Roxie Theater I had heard about. There were other places I had in mind, and then she said, "Where would you like to eat?"

"Well," I said, "I wouldn't know, but I've heard Jack Dempsey has a café here."

"Oh," she said, "that's fine."

Got all done, she gives three tickets for everything—it didn't cost anything—and I come back to the guys. They couldn't believe it, and we went to all that stuff. Every bit of it. And it didn't cost us a dime!

We got home that night and that guy that usually got plastered—he said, "Boy, I never believed a fella could see so much in one day in all my life!"

***

November 6, 1942: In a speech to the Congress of Soviet Deputies, Stalin warns the United States and Britain that "the absence of a seond front against Fascist Germany may end badly for all freedom-loving countries, including the Allies themselves." He declares that the aim of the coalition is "to save mankind from reversion to savagery and medieval brutality."

WWII Axis Military History Day-to-Day, www.feldgrall.com

Private Albrecht:
EUROPE OR PACIFIC

When basic training ended, we didn't know if we were going to Europe or Asia. It would be either one, but we didn't know which one. Nobody did. So often, if they trained you for cold weather, and you know that kind of stuff, well, then you would sure go to the Pacific where it was hotter than Sam Hill. If they trained you for the hot, you would go to the other place.

I was glad that we had to go to Europe rather than the Pacific. I don't know why. For some reason or other, I just didn't relish the idea of sneaking through a jungle. There in Europe we had the wide open spaces. The fellows from the Pacific would come home for a short leave, and then they would transfer them over to Europe. They didn't like it at all. They said, "Man alive, over here you're right out in the open—you got nothing to get behind. Over there we got jungle. You can hide, you know." We thought just the opposite. You would be in the jungle and all of a sudden you get an old spear sent through you or something—you didn't even see the guy. But I guess it's the way you get broken in.

When we were sent out to Meade and when we boarded ship at New York City, we figured then that we're going across the Atlantic. Otherwise, we'd have gone the other direction, like towards California or something like that. Then we were pretty sure that's where we would be heading. Course you never know in the Army. They could switch you and send you the other direction in a hurry.

Travel Day 1:
Across the Pond

The stewardess handed each of us a warm damp washcloth to freshen up before landing. An overnight flight can suit well-seasoned passengers who can doze off into a comfortable sleep, but for me, the fact that I was some-30,000 feet over the Atlantic in the dark of night for six-plus hours, kept my eyes at attention. I noticed Wilt and Dad nodding off from time to time, certainly with less worries, yet when we finally landed in Amsterdam, they too looked dragged out. An airplane seat just wasn't a bed.

Soldiers, well-armed, met us as we deplaned and entered the airport. Clearly on foreign soil now, we were at attention and ready to take on the adventure.

Our rental Ford Escort was up to the task but only with our bags carefully organized to fit the trunk and overflow into the back seat with me. I was comfortable to sit in the back slightly cross-wise for more leg room and more to the middle so that my conversation could be heard by both guys up front. Dad had no hearing in one ear and a hearing aid in the other.

From my back-seat position, I could navigate our route with spread-out maps and source books, and I could manage the hand-held voice recorder for capturing Dad's stories as we traveled from place to place. Wilt, of course, would have both eyes on the road. And Dad, we hoped, could sit back and soak in the sights.

Off we whisked into the thick of traffic. Heavy traffic, we soon caught on, would be a way of life for us the next ten days in this crowded country—crowded, as compared to our wide-open spaces back home in the upper Midwest. Large, fast trucks seemed to rule the freeways, keeping pace with the swift commuter traffic and commanding a threatening presence. And the town centers would pose a different yet equal challenge—there, the vehicles shared ridiculously tight streets with many, many pedestrians and many, many bicycles.

It was the *centrum* of Amsterdam where we were heading now as we left the airport—that's where we found the highly recommended canal tours. A leisurely jaunt in a canal tour boat seemed just the sort of sightseeing to start off our adventure. Even if the tour guide might fail to hold our interest, the boat ride itself would allow us time to recover a bit from our long flight. And it did. Having maneuvered in the car just that six-mile introduction to the roadways, we now could sit back in a comfortable boat and take in our new surroundings, free of the car.

What a sight of history unfolded, as if we were dropped into a different era: the centuries-old buildings, the cobblestones, the quaint shops, and bicycles galore. And there at the boat launch was a clue about Dutch history: a U.S. flag alongside the Dutch flag. We felt an immediate common bond in our new environment.

1992 – Canal tour boat in Amsterdam with two flags in the background, Dutch and U.S. (Author's Collection)

Still mesmerized by the boat ride and the picturesque surroundings, we eased off in our Escort again, refreshed and with calm resolve to locate, with little effort, accommodations for our first night. We estimated that Oosterhout might be a reasonable distance to allow early turn-in and a good night's sleep to make up for our shortage. The distance was correct on our part, but the matter of finding an accommodation would add an extra two hours to the calculation.

Importantly, and unaccounted for, part of the two hours was on foot as we combed a six-block area for an information center. Any on-foot diversions with travel itineraries can be most helpful for straightening the legs and refreshing the body, except when the distance drags on, and then drags on even more—especially so for a senior traveler. Dad, a slight man, nimble even at eighty-two, came back to the car dragging and puffing. If only we had packed one of those nifty collapsible stools, I scolded myself. Years later when accompanying Dad to his appointments at the VA Medical Center, I would reflect back on this trip when he showed the early effects of spinal stenosis and emphysema. For this day, he welcomed the car seat, and we made a mental pledge to assess surroundings before setting out on foot again.

Aside from that concern, the information center was worth the effort. A *pension* was what we were after, and the helpful guide suggested one within easy distance, as well as a restaurant in the same area, a perk that now had more meaning for us. Food and sleep, in that order were calling us, and we weren't going to be picky.

But even if our standards at that point had been high, The Eetcafe in Oosterhout surpassed them. The array of interesting vegetables especially grabbed my attention, and the guys enjoyed large portions of braised lamb, a dish not common back home. Sedated almost by the nourishing and relaxing meal, we shrugged off the fact that our bill was much more than we had budgeted. Oh, well, we agreed, we can make up the difference in our hotel.

And it was so that *Pension des ole Schurr* was economical. Our tour books and the information clerk had not steered us wrong—basic sleeping accommodations, clean, with a bathroom down the hall. The rooms were upstairs over *Schurr's* small restaurant and pub. That feature alone might have pushed us onward under other circumstances, but we stood firm in our decision. We were proud, savvy travelers to have found what we were after in keeping with our low-budget plan. Looking into the stark, cold rooms, however, we had little to say except, "At last, a place to sleep. This will work." After a quick, "Well, goodnight then, see you in the morning," Dad shuffled off to his room a couple doors down the hall. "Yes, Dad, see you in the morning. Just knock when you're up."

The knock came a little sooner than expected, 11:00 p.m., just three hours after we had turned in. Wilt jumped up, blurry-eyed, and opened the door a crack.

"Sorry to get you up, but I got to thinking that maybe I could get some sleep on that little couch you've got there?" Dad was pointing across the room and had a blanket and pillow in the other arm. "I remembered you had that. I'll bet I could get some sleep stretched out there—must be that my bed is too soft. Anyway, my legs have been aching and been giving me a hell of a time, probably from all that walking."

"Ah . . . sure, sure . . . come on in, Russ. Good idea. Give it a try!" Wilt eagerly grabbed Dad by the shoulder and pulled him in, as I scampered up to ready the new bed. Apparently we were relieved as well for all of us to be in close quarters this first night away in unaccustomed territory. "Should be warmer in here too with the three of us, brrr." Meanwhile downstairs in the little bar, musicians were striking up.

Amazingly, we all slept. The blaring of the band downstairs, which first shook our senses, faded by the power of much-needed sleep. When Wilt and I awoke at eight o'clock, Dad had already left the room. We found him downstairs enjoying a lively conversation with the owner who was frying an egg. Dad looked at home, even in the unusual surroundings of this little bar, and the two could have been best buddies, for a casual observer. "Oh, good morning, you two! I just talked Mr. Schurr here into frying me an egg. Otherwise, see there, the hardboiled eggs on the table? That's the usual, he says."

We eyed the table with cold breakfast choices and could imagine that Dad might be skeptical. Wilt gave me wink and whispered, "This is going to be a good trip."

***

September 18-19, 1944: Conversation between Roosevelt and Churchill at Hyde Park, September 18, 1944: "The suggestion that the world should be informed regarding TulBE AL.OYs, with a view to an international agreement regarding its control and use, is not accepted. The matter should continue to be regarded as of the utmost secrecy; but when a 'bomb' is finally available, it might perhaps, after mature consideration, be used against the Japanese, who should be warned that this bombardment will be repeated until they surrender."

***

Post-Conference Conversations at Hyde Park—Editorial Note "The Churchill party left Hyde Park at 10:30 p.m., September 19, traveling by train to New York, where they boarded the *Queen Mary* for the trip back to England."

U.S. Department of State/Foreign Relations of the U.S.
Conference at Quebec, 1944, www.digicoll.library.wisc.edu

Private Albrecht:
THE QUEEN MARY & CHURCHILL

We went over on the Queen Mary—*left September the twentieth from New York City. We didn't know what ship it was. We came on there at night, loaded on a big ship, we knew that. I was on B Deck. There was like a stateroom, normally for two people, but all the furniture was out and there were bunks up the side. Thirteen of us were in there.*

The Queen Mary *and the* Queen Elizabeth *were the two largest ships afloat and the biggest load the* Queen Mary *ever carried I guess was 17,000 on one trip. I imagine we probably had 12,000 to 13,000 when I went over, and of course, like I say, we didn't know what ship it was.*

When we got in our stateroom, we had orders that that's where you stay, and you stay in there until you are given authority to come out, which wouldn't be until the next day. Well, we felt the ship move and right away rumors spread— which you get used to in the Army—somebody said, "We're on the Queen Mary!"

Well, if that's the case, so what?

All of a sudden it stopped. "We're stopping at Ellis Island—we're picking up Churchill! He was here visiting our president and he's getting on!"

Well, we took that with a grain of salt. Every room had a loud speaker and then the next morning all of a sudden that speaker system blared open—the first thing in the morning: "Private Russel Albrecht"—and some other person— "report to the captain!"

Well, holy smokes, you know, I couldn't figure what in the Sam Hill was the matter. Everybody looked at me and said, "What the heck did you do?"

Well, I said, "I don't know. I didn't do anything." Well then I figured that maybe something had happened to Lorraine or one of the kids, and that's the only way they could contact me, you know, by radio or whatever on the ship.

The ship was divided in three sections—red, white, and blue. Whatever section you were in you got a big button, and you had to have that on your uniform. If you had a white button, that's the section you're in, and you don't go in the blue or the red. That's forbidden. So anyway, we had to find the captain— this other fella, I don't know what outfit he was from, but I had never seen him before. Anyway, he and I finally found the captain of the ship. And here, he and I were made MPs!

Me of all people—about probably the oldest one of our bunch and small, I mean not a great big guy. We were given a carbine and told that every morning from 8:00 to 10:00 we guard the promenade deck. That's the big deck that runs all the way around the ship. There are dozens and dozens of doors going on to it. Well, they were all locked except the main door, big doors there. They couldn't lock those because if something happened to the ship, you know, nobody could get off. So I was on the starboard, and the other guy was on the port side.

The captain said, "Churchill and his wife and daughter and his royal guards will take their morning walk from 8:00 to 10:00, and you guard that entry onto the promenade deck. Nobody, no matter how much brass he has got on his shoulder, goes out there, no matter who, because," he said, "I am captain of the boat and nobody has anything to say but me!"

Well, that sounded kind of good, you know, being just a plain private. So we took our positions that next morning at eight o'clock. We waited a while, and pretty soon here come Churchill and his wife and daughter and royal guards. They took a morning walk, and it took them about two hours. They would mess around going around on that walk. Then the second morning they stopped, and he came over to me and wanted to know where I was from and some of that stuff and then moved on. And, of course, all this time there was a lot of officers on board from different units, and they all wanted to get out on there and meet Churchill. But of course we couldn't let them out. That was kind of fun when a guy came with a bunch of stars on, and we said, "I'm sorry, sir, but you can't go out there."

Why in the world they picked me, I'll never know, but they did. On the fourth day Churchill stopped again, and I met his wife and his daughter, and he talked a little more about my being married and the kids. His wife and daughter didn't say anything—they were just standing there listening, but Churchill seemed nice. He had that big long cigar like you always see him with and that voice that he had. Seemed interested, and he said, "Don't forget that the British also have troops over there." In other words, we shouldn't think we're doing the whole thing. He made that plain.

By the way, we had an escort when we left New York—two destroyers and a cruiser. Every seven minutes we would change course because it took a submarine ten minutes to get a bead on you, and by the time they got a bead, you had already turned. Well, when we got halfway across the Atlantic, then our three [escort] ships turned around and went back home, and the British met us with the same kind of ships and took us the rest of the way up into Scotland. That was for Churchill. Otherwise, the Queen never had an escort, or it was very, very seldom they would have an escort. Then when we got, I suppose, a day from the British Isles, then we had an umbrella of airplanes over us practically all the time, British airplanes. That was, of course, for Churchill's protection.

Well, then on the fifth day, we come up on the Firth of Clyde. As we come into Scotland, then the ship stopped, and a couple of tugs came out with a big fence, or whatever. It was underwater—went all the way across that Clyde.

One tug would get a hold of one side and one the other, and they pulled it apart just so we could sneak through with the Queen. As soon as we were through, boy, they went right back and closed it up. That was so no submarines could come up in there. The British kept a lot of their aircraft carriers and other war ships up there in the Firth of Clyde, which was a big stream going up into Scotland.

Then we went up as far as I think Greenock, and we anchored out in the middle because the Queen took up too much space on the dock. Then first Churchill's yacht came out and put the gangplank across. Then his royal guards, with some help from some GIs, carried stuff that he had gotten in the U.S.—hatboxes the women had, and Churchill had boxes of liquor and you name it. They carried until I thought they were going to sink that yacht. Then finally when they got done, then Churchill used the speaker connected with the system on the ship and talked to everybody, a little talk, and then they left.

Well, then the landing boats came over, we got on them, and they took us on to shore. There we got on a train and went into Glasgow, Scotland. I think we stayed in the cars we were in, but we were there probably an hour and they got us turned around with a different engine or two, and then we started down through England and through London. We came to a camp, and there we unloaded and were for the night. We were in England just overnight, you might say. We had one good chicken dinner there. That cook seemed to know how to make something. Of course, he was an American.

Travel Day 2:
Petite Café

NAIVETÉ CAN BE USEFUL IN ACHIEVING results, when full knowledge of circumstances might put the damper on ambitions. You just can't mind looking foolish every now and again. That's what I usually take away from our free-spirit approach to travel. Does it matter really that the serene country roads you envisioned really are congested highways with speeding semis? Just slow down, appreciate the commercial activity. And who cares how many times you need to ask for directions? Sometimes those conversations are comic relief. Furthermore, if an accommodation doesn't exactly meet your budget, can't you make up the difference down the road? Well, maybe, maybe not. The point is you figure it all out on the spot.

Unfortunate for my dad though, with more of a mind to plan perfectly, all ducks in a row, he had to learn this free-spirited approach on the go. But he didn't point a finger and didn't complain, although at times I did notice a raised eyebrow, a nervous clearing of the throat, a general uneasiness in the passenger seat.

Mostly, he channeled his opinions into humor, with a teaching point for good measure. For instance, he might say after we had miscalculated the driving time which meant a delay in finding a hotel for the night, "Sure glad I'm with you two experienced travelers—otherwise, I'd be worried about where we're going to sleep . . . yup, *I'm* not worried." Then he'd give us a glance, and we would grin.

"Well, that's good, Dad. Who needs sleep anyway?"

And that's how it went as Wilt and I scrambled to make the trip come off without a slip. After all, well-meaning friends had warned that including a senior on such a trip might cause a health set-back. We had reason to scramble. And, remember, I was hoping for the perfect trip.

For this day, the 350 miles or so between Oosterhout, our overnight in the Netherlands, to Deauville on the coast of France, would be easy enough for one day and allow time for plenty of stops along the way. That's what we figured. But our preview just the day before on that first day of driving should have given us a clue—the heavily traveled highways *then* were still slow *today*.

Thanks to Wilt's steady hand at the wheel and our overall high expectations as foreigners ready to learn, we barreled along refreshed and eager to take it all in. The countryside was beautiful in its density with steeples and colorful rooftops, and Dad was quick to point out that the towns in Holland were exceptionally neat. "Yup, that's why I always liked Holland. They sure keep things tidy." As kids, my sisters and I had this cultural lesson drilled-in as an example of how we might one day tend to our homes. So now actually here in Holland, I watched specifically for any messy yards, debris, clutter, even a slip of paper loose along the roadway. He was right.

Belgium had a similar feel except minus canals. Relative to our wide open spaces back home, crossing a country and then into the next within just a half-day gave us a distorted sense of speed, even though we fully realized that the thick traffic was slowing us down. "Gosh, Belgium already?" Dad pointed out as he noticed a sign. That positive note on our progress was enough to suggest finding a good place for a break.

The city of Kortrijk, we decided, fit perfectly on our allotted time for a stretch and a bite to eat. But, like in Amsterdam, finding the center of town was where we veered off course. Blame it on all of the narrow one-way streets, the distraction of bicyclists everywhere it seemed, the signage we didn't always understand. That's where asking for directions comes in handy.

Finally, landing at a café, we caught our breaths. A little debriefing along the way we learned was always good with Dad over a cup of coffee. Caffeine for him seemed to settle his nerves. "Yah," he said relaxing back in his chair, "I'm glad we'll circle back to Holland before we leave. I really liked that, you betcha." Wilt and I filed that thought away in our "good-trip-for-Dad" bank. And on that note, we leisurely finished our lunch, now able to laugh at all our wrong turns.

Our next stop some two hours down the road was a church, and not just any centuries-old European church—this was the *famous* Amiens Cathedral built in the thirteenth century. With its stone-vaulted nave reaching a height of 138.8 feet, it is known as the tallest complete cathedral in all of France. Taking it all in—the spires, the sculpture, the sheer mass of this old structure—we began to feel the impact of being far, far away on foreign soil. Indeed, we were in a history lesson. For Dad, who compared all things to back home, it was the height which impressed him. With a calculating eye, he stood looking up at the dome. "You know, that ceiling there is even taller than Morgan's water tower. Can you believe that?"

It was after the church that we found another café, this time just for coffee. That's when we learned that here in France a tasty cookie accompanied the coffee order for "*petite café.*" That's also when Dad took a new appreciation for his bottomless cup back home at the Morgan Pool Hall and the fact that there a cup of coffee was only twenty-five cents. The *petite café* went down fast. Those tiny cups with the hearty espresso should have signaled an appropriate sipping, but soon Dad had his cup raised for a refill.

"*Oui, oui,*" the waitress smiled with a questioning look, then darted to the kitchen. It was a fresh new set that she hurried back to Dad—cookie and extra charge included.

"Well I'll be darned," he shook his head, "guess these French people don't know about refills." He drank down half the cup. "Here, you two can have my extra cookie." Then he sipped the last drops from the miniature cup.

Now closing in on late afternoon, we hit the road again. Just a couple more hours, we added up from the map, and we would find a nice hotel near the coast, have a relaxing dinner, and be ready for our next big day at Omaha Beach. We didn't know then that our coffee and cookies in Amiens would have to last us until nearly ten o'clock that night.

The closer we got to the coastal region, the thicker the traffic. A bit more research on our part would have clued us in about the elite tourist attraction where we were heading: Deauville. Regarded as the "Queen of the Norman beaches," Deauville claims to be one of the most prestigious seaside resorts in all of France. Here we were, fresh from Minnesota's heartland in hopes of an economy hotel in this vacationland of the elite.

How we ever found the Open Hotel with its doable rate of one hundred dollars for the two rooms, remains a mystery. I do recall vividly circling the blocks of posh hotels. Now the hour was late, daylight gone, a chilling drizzle. In desperation, I boldly walked into several of these distinguished accommodations with the blind hope that somehow I could find a deal, here among the rich and famous. After each humiliating encounter, I ducked back to the car, shook my head "No!" and we proceeded in silence through traffic around another block.

So the Open Hotel, stark as it was on the outskirts of town, offered just what we needed: rest. Though we still didn't have adaptable plug-ins, we did have heat. And the in-hotel café meant we did not have to get back in the car that day. "Mixed grill" is what suited Wilt from the menu, while Dad and I settled on a comforting tomato soup. Dead tired but relaxed now that we were fed and had a place to sleep, we lingered at the table to go over the day's events. What was most on Dad's mind? The French idea for a decent cup of coffee: Petite café.

Finding Foxholes

***

September 14, 1944: The Great Atlantic Hurricane makes landfall in the New York City area. *Hurricane Science and Society, www.hurricanescience.org*

Private Albrecht:
OMAHA BEACH

The next day in England we went over to, I think, South Hampton where we boarded a liberty ship, one that we had given to the Dutch—the Dutch were in charge of it anyway. That's what we went across the Channel on. It was one of those, you know, that the Americans made in a hurry. They were made for quick use, and they looked like they'd bust in half in a high sea—but we had that.

We had a lot of wind on the Channel, but we went across and got over by Omaha Beach. We couldn't go over to the shore because everything was busted up already with no docks or anything. It was rougher than the dickens so the ship stayed out, and then they brought some landing barges out to take us into shore. But it was so rough that the barges would hit the shipside, and they were splintering up.

They had to quit and wait. I don't remember how long we waited on there, probably eight to ten hours, then finally they got orders from shore, "You get them guys on shore right now. We need them and no more waiting!"

Well, then they came out with the landing barges, and they put long rope ladders and stretched 'em quite a ways away. Then we all lined up on the ship along the side—two lines, one from each direction. We met there where the rope ladder was, and then four guys would go down at a time. Some of the rungs were broken out, and you know how rope is to crawl. And then you are over real rough water, and you had a full field pack on, your overcoat, your rifle over your shoulder, everything. You get on that rope and you tip sideways, and on the edges the guy would tip—well, if you tipped, you really had to grip or do something to get back up. Otherwise, in the drink you went. If you did, that was it. Well, I saw three guys when I came walking along on my side that tipped over, and, blump, in they went and that was the end of 'em. You got all the weight on, and you didn't come up and nobody even looked for you. It was too rough.

I was just hopin' and prayin' I wouldn't get on the outside edge, but doggone *it, I did. I got about halfway down to the landing boat, and then I tipped over. I don't know how I got back up, but I sure did. I think my finger marks are still on that rope!*

But I got down there and got on that landing barge, and then they brought us in to shore. There we had a little narrow path the engineers had made that was mine-free—probably about four feet wide. We followed that up to some trucks.

Over this landing area we had these barrage balloons up—great big, oh, like dirigibles with cables on. They were big balloons, but they had a lot of sections to 'em. By having that where we'd land, the German planes couldn't come swooping in and machine gun anybody—because they'd hit those cables. They would shoot at the balloons, but there were more compartments so just one or two blasts in one wouldn't make it come down.

I don't remember the date we landed. We were replacements, you see— I wasn't in the Thirtieth then. We were assigned that after we got on. We were called replacements—our whole boatload. Then we joined the Division.

From the day I left New York City until we had our foxhole blown all to smithereens on the Front, it was ten days. It took us five days to come over, so it was five days from when we landed in Scotland until getting' right up to the Front.

***

1944: "First, the replacement system rushed men into combat without adequate preparation and created an unnecessary arduous challenge of adjustment on the field of battle . . . Second, the small number of divisions required units to remain in the front lines without rest and beyond the limits of individual human endurance, thus causing an earlier than necessary breakdown of veterans whose invaluable combat experience and skills were lost prematurely."

Army History, Prof. Francis Steckel, U.S. Army Center of Military History, 1994

***

"It was not the job of the front-line machine gunner or tanker to train replacements. The Army was supposed to do that, and it failed."

Stephen Ambrose, *Citizen Soldiers* (Simon & Schuster, 1997)

Private Albrecht:

GREENHORNS

From Omaha Beach we were hauled in trucks. We went a ways the first time we stopped. We were getting a lot of rain, and there was a big ridge with a bunch of pine trees on it. Of course, we didn't see that because it was dark, but it was low ground there, and that was supposed to be the area to stop for the night. We had a captain and a lieutenant in charge of us. They called it "the package," and on the boat coming over they were in charge of us. We stopped that night and they said, "Okay, here's where you get out to pitch your tents."

Well, we looked and that whole area—like a pasture or whatever—it probably had two to three inches of water on it all over. "Well, where should we pitch?"

"Oh, right there, that's where you pitch."

He was a nut, he and his lieutenant. His name was Captain Fowler. I will never forget that. We had to go out and pitch those pup tents in the water and, not only that, then go in and lay in it—and that was a must. *He came along with a flashlight, which he wasn't even supposed to have because they told us just over the next hill, that's the enemy. We never knew where the heck they were. Anyway, we all got soaked of course laying in that stuff. Come morning, here was that nice big ridge right next to us with those pine trees. We could have all been up there on high ground.*

Then there was—oh, it would be like a pole barn now that we have here—a bunch of poles up with a roof over, and there was a sergeant he had in charge of that thing. That was a place where you could get some food. We went up for breakfast, and he couldn't get over it that we would pitch the tents down in that water. "Well," we said, "there was no choice. That was the orders."

Nobody was allowed to put a shell in his gun either. If the captain would catch you with a rifle loaded, you would get court martialed.

"Anyway," he said, "you guys come on up and get something to eat. There's a little town just a half mile from here. Would you like to take a hike? I'll take you guys, and we'll hike into town. Being you were in that water, it will do you good. Otherwise you're going to get all stiffened up."

"Ya," we all agreed to that. So he took us into this town just to march in there, and then we rested for a while and then started back.

Well, then about that time here comes our lieutenant and the captain in a Jeep. He saw us, and he recognized us and stopped. Oh, he started chewing out this sergeant for taking us out. He said, "You have no authority to do that!" Then that sergeant let him know in one short order who was boss around there when anybody stopped in that place, and definitely the captain wasn't. So he finally left us alone.

Here's something else we learned—down at the end of the orchard they had dug a straddle trench, that's your latrine, biff, in other words. I was down there squatting over that doggone straddle trench, doing what I came there for, and all of a sudden somebody tapped me on the shoulder. Here's a lady *standing there right by me with a basket on her arm, and she had some pears and some apples in there which they raised right there. She wanted to give me some. Man alive, you know, that surprised me so I didn't know what the heck, if I should go down and fall in the hole or stand up or keep on doin' what I was doin' or what! I kind of looked at her, "No, no, no, get out of here—I don't want any apples or whatever!"*

She kind of looked so funny at me like, "Well, what's the matter with you?" She was going to be so nice to me.

I went back and told one of the guys in charge, "Say, you got to get some canvas and put up around that straddle trench. Cripes, I was sittin' over there and a lady *came over!"*

"Oh, no, no, you don't need anything here—that's nothing. They're used to that. You just go wherever you feel like it. That's all right."

That was a little hard to get used to!

Anyway, they loaded us on trucks and we went up another way. All of a sudden they stopped—and Frances Albee, from south of Chicago, and me—they called our two names. We got off and the guy said, "Now, you start walkin' down the road and somebody will meet you down there." We didn't know anything, but you had to do what you were supposed to, so we did. The truck moved on with the rest of the guys.

Well, we found out that we were replacements for a couple of guys that got nailed in the Division and that's when we got in the Thirtieth Division. Pretty soon here comes a guy walkin' up the road, a corporal or somebody. "Oh, here you are," we said, "You're the guy we're supposed to meet?"

"Yup, just follow me." We stayed right behind him. "Oh, wait a minute, wait a minute, get farther apart!" he said. "If a shell comes in, it won't get all of us."

Then we knew we were up there where it was bad. Pretty soon I said, "Say, Corporal, when do we load these things?"

Man, he stopped right there. He says, "Load them—don't tell me you're coming around here with an empty rifle!"

"Well," I said, "we had orders if we put a shell in there without authority, we can get court marshaled."

"Well," he said, "what kind of a duck got a hold of you guys?! You load them and don't ever *leave 'em unloaded! From now on you be ready to use it any minute!"*

Well, then we walked apart and got up to a barn, a big brick one that had some water around, a little bridge goin' over to it, and then there was an orchard next to it with a big hedge around it. We were actually northeast of Aachen. That was high ground and we were supposed to hold that. We got through that orchard and there was an old house pretty well beat up and a plain field with a couple of live pillboxes that were in the Siegfried Line.

We went in this old house in the basement and there was a lieutenant and his medic. It was a CP, Command Post. This corporal said to the lieutenant, "Well, here are your two men."

I can tell you now you didn't call him "Lieutenant"—we called him "Pepsi," and that's what this guy said—"Pepsi, here's your two men." The reason was when you're on the Front Line you don't salute nobody. You don't wear any pins that show you're lieutenant or colonel or whatever you are. You don't call anybody "Sir." That's because if the Germans are watching, they look for an officer, and if you salute somebody, that's the guy they're going to nail first. That was a no, no. When you get back on a rest or something, fine, go ahead and salute and do your honors, but not up there.

The lieutenant and his men in the basement, they looked us two over. He kind of shook his head and then this medic says, "Oh, oh . . . cannon fodder."

That didn't sound very good. He asked us what our ages were. This Albee was I guess thirty-two or somethin' like that, and then I was goin' on thirty-five.

"Oh, oh . . . cannon fodder."

What they wanted was some young guys.

"You go over there in the orchard and dig a hole."

Up until this time, when we dug a hole somebody told you where to dig it. I said, "Well, where do we dig it?"

"Go over there and don't get right next to somebody else—see where they are and get in between there."

Okay, so we went over and dug a hole—or started to dig it. It was in an orchard and there were these fruit trees in there—pear trees, apple trees—and there was some fruit on. So, we would dig a little bit and then we would get a pear and sit on the edge of the hole and eat it.

All of a sudden we heard this whistle of artillery shell coming . . . boom! It went over the orchard, of course, not right there. Well, we got used to that overhead artillery. I said, "We're shooting at somebody, I suppose. We don't need to worry about that."

Pretty soon another one came and boom!—that was closer. I wondered, "Is that enemy gettin' closer or what?"

We weren't in any hurry getting our hole dug. We were eating an apple, and then all of a sudden a shell came in and, man, that came in right close and the crap flew, dirt flew! We looked and I said, "I suppose that's a short round."

"Yah," Albee said.

Pretty soon some other GI stuck his head out. He said, "What the hell's the matter with you guys? Why in the hell didn't you get down?"

We said, "Isn't that our artillery?"

"Our artillery? Hell no—that's German!"

Boy, I tell you that hole got dug fast. That dirt was really flying. We got a hole we could get into, and from then on we knew what the score was. Nobody tells you a doggone thing. You learn from experience.

1944 – "Seldom did our men at Birk dare leave their foxholes. (History of the 120th Infantry Regiment)

Travel Day 3:
Taking France

WE AWOKE TO A SUNNY DAY, which was reason enough to get on the road early, eager to get to the actual starting point of Dad's experience on enemy territory. Our trip so far was just to position ourselves at the beginning of our detective work. From Normandy Beach on, we would be more or less tracking Dad's route.

The Open Hotel café wasn't, well, *open* at that hour so we imagined a breakfast stop on the way. But once again we were overly optimistic with travel times, somehow neglecting to consider the heavy traffic in this popular region of France. The city of Caen is a destination in itself. And as our route took us closer to the coast, the roads narrowed and traffic slowed. Also, we were overly optimistic about roadside eating establishments. This country rich with gourmet tradition dating back centuries was not about to offer up a Country Kitchen just for convenience.

So, it wasn't until eleven o'clock that we finally found breakfast, and then it was only coffee with bread and jam. "Gosh darn it, doesn't anyone here know about toast?" Dad looked almost as if he would refuse the bread, but after second thoughts, he wolfed it down and looked for more. This was at a gas station offering a small sit-down area for refreshments. But unlike our store-bought, nutrient-lacking versions at home, here the bread was fresh and crusty, the jam like Grandma's, and the coffee brewed bold. The $6.00 per order raised our eyebrows but only slightly. After all, we were in search of food.

The wind had picked up with a sky of big patchy gray clouds when we arrived at Normandy Beach. The air had a chill. The parking lot at the site was almost empty, which was odd in light of the traffic we just escaped. And the beach, too, was vacant.

As if to confirm that we were, in fact, at the right location, Dad announced, "Well, this is the place all right," as he zipped up his jacket and grabbed for his camera.

The broad expanse of cliff facing the English Channel left nothing to argue that the Allies performed what could have been an insurmountable task on that day of invasion, June 6, 1944. The Germans positioned in their "resistance nests," massive concrete bunkers built on top of the cliffs, had the upper hand. Some 2,400 Americans fell. But by the end of the day, 34,000 troops had been landed, and the Allies had secured the beachhead. Now forty-eight years later here we stood as tourists, one having walked these cliffs in 1944.

It wasn't at the invasion but nearly three months after that Dad landed here—he as one of the thousands of "replacements" to fill the holes in ranks left by the dead. Demand for replacements after the invasion was urgent due to the high rate of casualties: ninety percent in the infantry divisions alone! One would have good reason to worry about the psyche of these men filling slots, "orphans" as they were called. Some thought of themselves as replaceable parts. But Uncle Sam needed riflemen, and that was the assignment for Private First Class Russel E. Albrecht.

As Dad described his landing on that day in September 1944—the hurried-up orders, the wildly choppy sea, the rope ladders stretching to landing barges, soldiers dropping out of sight—one has a glimpse into the complexities of staging troops. Waiting for calmer waters wasn't an option with soldier-power in drastic short supply. And what was to become of these replacement soldiers, so minimally trained, as they climbed the cliffs of Omaha Beach and stepped foot into enemy territory?

I stood at the crest of the bluff and had the sensation of dropping into another time, as if peering into a tragic scene from long ago, now washed clean of

1992 – Omaha Beach. ((Author's Collection)

its atrocities. The heavy clouds, the cold wind, and the dark waves seemed to have witnessed the events. I wondered, is the beach empty because of the chilly conditions or is it empty simply in tribute to this old soldier? I think it was the latter.

Dad tightened down his cap, pulled up his jacket collar and began the descent to the beach. His nimble legs, even with a slight hitch to his gait, defied his eighty-two years. I tried to keep up, but his pace quickened. At the water's edge, he took long strides as if he intended to walk the entire length of the six-mile beach.

"Dad, check out this rock," I hollered to get his attention. He stopped to look back and then as if refocused to the present, he looked down and then stooped to pick up a rock of his own.

"Just look at this one, Faye," he said as I caught up to him. "It's so smooth and clean from that ocean washing over it all those years. Yup, that Channel is a rough one, that's for sure." He turned the stone over and over in his hands to show me, and then he slipped it into his pocket. Then we stared out at the surging waves.

Wilt had been busy with the camera and the memorials, and it was this that finally tore us from the mesmerizing ocean and the smooth stones. The sun peeking out at intervals warmed us enough to linger as we read the history and absorbed the importance of this place. Dad studied long the 1944 map and beach depiction labeled "Omaha: *Le Succes*." "That's right," he said, "it was a success."

1992 – Dad walking the cliffs at Omaha Beach. (Author's Collection)

Now back in the car and heading out, we paused again: There on the bluff overlooking Omaha Beach was the Normandy American Cemetery and Memorial. The field of white crosses mark the over 9,000 American military dead, most killed during the invasion of Normandy and the following battles. "It makes a guy think, doesn't it?" That's all Dad had to say. Wilt shifted the car to drive, and we continued on, a good while in silence.

Paris was our destination for the night, which was a formidable task in itself, knowing what I know now. This again was where free-spirit trip planning came up. The distance wasn't the problem, just little more than a two-hour drive, but the know-how on accommodations once we got there was. The toll road thankfully shot us across the French countryside. Wait. French countryside isn't where a traveler should be "shot across," lovely as it is. A traveling shame, you might say. Friends who have toured France on bicycles savored every scene. But keep in mind, *our* trip was about covering a lot of territory quickly in search of remembrances for our old soldier. His thinking was all about 1944. And so far, Wilt and I were a bit anxious.

Lucky for us and quite unintentionally, just before hitting the toll road, we happened upon one of those remembrances also natural to the French countryside. We found ourselves on one of the "sunken roads" that Dad described.

"See there," Dad pointed out the window at the high embankments on each side of the road. "That's how some of those German tankers could hide." Stopping then and walking alongside one of these high embankments, we understood completely. And now we had the perspective of a foot soldier.

1992 – "Sunken road" typical to Normandy region. (Author's Collection)

That perspective, that sense of what this trip was about, was good to keep in mind when we hit the outskirts of bustling Paris just before sunset. We needed food and rest to sharpen our focus for the next day, and Paris, we agreed, was just going to be a stopping point. The General Hospital that Dad recalled, if it, in fact, still existed, would have meant at least a full day in Paris. Maybe, we thought, we can hit Paris again on our way back.

That idea quickly soured as we began this search for a hotel and encountered the locals. Granted, the time was late, we were tired and hungry, and traffic was heavy, yesterday's scenario all over again. We vowed then to plan better. And now in asking for directions, even our most kindly Minnesota manner seemed to encourage the *opposite* in response. "Hey, how about a minute to spare for us out-of-towners?" That's what we should have said. "Never mind that we can't speak your language." I was reminded of the light-hearted advice about Paris from a travel-savvy friend: "Be rude—you are in Paris after all!" Whoa, that's not how I was raised.

The man who finally did offer helpful advice we wondered later might have been tipsy. He surely was smiley with a faint whiff of alcohol. But his directions were sound, and we were thankful to end up at the Eco Motel, well within our budget as the name implied. The rooms were comfortable and even were equipped with electrical outlets appropriate for Dad's razor. He beamed when he showed up at our room later with a clean shaven face. "Now that's more like it," he said, smoothing his chin.

Little did we know then that soon after World War II, this neighborhood of Paris known as St. Germain became a hotspot for intellectuals and philosophers, actors and musicians. The likes of Picasso hung out here. And it continues as a tourist destination with museums, art dealers, galleries, and fashionable restaurants, all tucked in around centuries-old churches—this was a renaissance of a sort after the war. So, you see, unknowingly, we had a small connection back to the era of World War II here in this neighborhood of the humble Eco Motel.

The Court Paille down the block, which offered grilled meats and fries, didn't offer a clue that we might be in a fashionable eating spot. But then, our focus was narrow. Ever mindful of our eighty-two-year-old travel companion, Wilt and I tended to opt for convenience and comfort in any of our trip decisions. If it wasn't a place Dad could walk to, food he would enjoy, or memory he would savor, forget it. On the other hand, he likely would have made the best out of any direction we chose, even enjoyed it. That was how he operated. Yet, I had to worry.

On our walk back to the motel, we stopped for a couple of minutes to observe the pleasant surroundings at a bridge over the river in the neighborhood. How nice, we thought. Very nice. Had we been in another mode, the Seine River absolutely would have been a highlight, a place to linger—this was another one of those travel destinations we just bumbled across. I expect that one day Wilt and I will return to Paris and to that very place on the Seine and give the city its due. But for this trip—this experience—my journal says it best at the close of the day when the three of us sat in our room at the Eco Motel playing cards: "Played cards, 'Widow,' until ten thirty. Hope to get out of France tomorrow."

***

November 16, 1944: "My Day" by Eleanor Roosevelt—"When shopping in New York the other day, I went in to America House where I saw Mrs. Vanderbilt Webb. She told me of a very interesting plan which is being developed by Dartmouth College in cooperation with the American Craftsmen's Educational Council, Inc . . . They are working out with the Veterans Administration a way in which veterans wishing to take advantage of this plan may do so. The plan is designed to give men and women training in careers as craftsmen. Every step is pointed to one end, the financial independence of the individual, either through self-employment or employment in the manual industries. The course of instruction, given at Dartmouth College is open to men and women, both civilians and returning veterans. Those who are disabled or suffering from combat neurosis may also take advantage of it. Since handicraft production is usually easier to carry out in rural communities, the plan should be of special interest to those who may wish to settle in the country . . ."

George Washington University, The Published and Recorded Works of Eleanor Roosevelt, www.gwu.edu

Private Albrecht:
THE SUMP HOLE, THE WHEAT STACK, AND PIGEONS

We stayed at that orchard for some time and got shelled day in and day out. The Germans figured that we had a bunch of tanks and stuff back in that orchard, and they were blasting. But there weren't any. We had a big mortar battalion back in there with big mortars, but that was it.

The town right across, Euchen, that was a strong SS place. That's where the stuff was coming from. Of course, the field between us and them was probably 900 feet—and there was this wheat stack. We had a hole on each end of that wheat stack, and four guys went out there every day in the morning and came back before dark. A telephone was out there, and we would watch the Germans and call back and tell what was going on.

First, I had to go out there, not Albee. We had so damn much water in our hole from raining all the time—had a couple of inches—and you had to lay in that dang stuff. So, I said, "We'll make a sump hole."

Albee was not much of an outdoors guy or anything—never had too much to do with that, I guess. Well, he says, "I'll dig that hole while you're gone."

1944 – "Communications and control were difficult to maintain." (History of the 120th Infantry Regiment)

"No," I said, "just leave the doggone thing. Go over in the barn—you can stay there during the day while I'm out there."

"No, I'll dig that hole."

"No," I argued.

Finally, "Well . . . okay then."

We went over towards the barn with the water around and the little bridge going over. We just got to the little bridge when the shells came in, and we had to hit the ground. They blew close to us, but we didn't pay attention. Albee went in the barn. I went out and got the other guy to go with me, and we ran out to our wheat stack.

Then in the evening before dark, we came back, and Albee was in the barn yet. Then he and I went over to the hole. Here our hole had got blown all to smithereens! We got a direct hit right in it! Albee looked at that and he said, "Albrecht, I'll never argue with you again!" He would have been in there digging that sump hole.

A few days later, we had to go out again to the wheat stack, this time Albee too. That's when these pigeons were sitting on there eating that wheat. Every time a shell would come by, they would raise up, you know. Of course, I could imagine eating some pigeon, so I told Albee, "Don't move a damn muscle."

I shelled out some wheat in my hand and brought it out by the hole. Pretty soon a pigeon came along there eating that up. When he got close enough, I quick grabbed him and tore his head and skin off and took him apart. We had some little cellophane bags, sort of, that some of our rations came in so I shoved the pigeon in there, and Albee put that in his pocket. Then I told him to be quiet. Another one came, and I caught that one. I did the same thing. I said, "When we get back tonight, we'll light our K-ration boxes." They had so much wax on they'd stay lit like a candle pretty near. We could put the blanket over the top of our hole and light those boxes down in there. The light wouldn't show up, and we could hold that pigeon over the fire and eat some pigeon.

But, before we had a chance to come back in from the wheat pile, jeez, we got a whole bunch of shelling. It knocked out our telephones, and then of course we couldn't come back because nobody told us to. You didn't come back on your own—you had to wait 'til you got orders to come. It got rainy and windy, kind of a miserable evening. It got dark, and finally about ten o'clock the signal corps got our phones working, and they said, "Well, come on back, but stay far apart."

So we came back, but we stayed together because it was so dang dark you couldn't see nothing. We got to the hedge around our orchard, and we couldn't find the opening. It was a real thick hedge—you didn't just walk through it. Finally, somebody found us and hollered, so we all went over there.

We just got inside the hedge, and they started shelling us again. So we hit the ground right in back of the hedge. Pretty soon one came in and landed, oh, probably ten feet from the hedge right by us, laying there—all four of us. I was the second guy from the left, and all three of those guys got hit—and I didn't! It tore our clothes and stuff like that—the helmet blew off—but they were all hit, including Albee.

They were yelling and rolling around, and I ran across the road to the CP where the lieutenant and the medic were. We got some help and got those three down in the basement, and the medic started working on them. Then they got some guys and some stretchers. They had to carry them about a half-mile or something like that before a vehicle would come up there to pick them up. So those guys took them off.

The lieutenant couldn't figure how come I wasn't hit. "You peel down— you got to be hit some place."

I peeled down, and there weren't cuts any place, just probably black and blue a place or two.

Then I was going to go back to the hole. "No," he said, "you find a corner here on the floor, roll down there, and stay there for the night." Then he went and got his whiskey—they always got a ration. He poured some.

I never was much on whiskey and I said, "No, I don't care for it."

He said, "This is an order—now drink it!"

So I did. Then I lay down and, oh, along about four o'clock in the morning I heard the guys come back that carried the fellows. I heard them say something about "Albrecht." I didn't know what he was saying until it got light, and then the lieutenant came and said, "Here, one of the fellows sent this back. Your buddy said you're going to need it worse than he does."

Albee was sending back his pigeon that he had in his pocket! So, I had two pigeons.

Finding Foxholes

***

1944: "Powers of Good—With every power for good to stay and guide me, comforted and inspired beyond all fear, I'll live these days with you in thought beside me, and pass, with you, into the coming year!"

Dietrich Bonhoeffer and Wayne Witson Floyd, *The Wisdom and Witness of Dietrich Bonhoeffer*, Augsburg Fortress, 2000.

Private Albrecht:
THE ATHEIST

After Albee, I got a new guy for the hole. He was an atheist. I didn't know him yet just that he was going to be my partner in the hole. Right away, of course, the next day we started getting the heck shelled out of us again. You wouldn't even want to stick your head out of the hole—or go out there to get an apple or a pear, because, remember, we were in the orchard—the shells were coming in too fast.

I was reading my little Testament, and he says, "What you reading there?"

"Oh," I said, "the Testament."

"Oh, you believe in that stuff, too?"

"Well," I said, "that's why I'm reading it."

"Well, that's a bunch of hooey. That's all that is. It doesn't mean a thing."

"How come?"

"Oh, heck," he said, "I went to church once in my life. I think I was about six or seven years old, with my folks, and that's the last time. That's just a bunch of gook."

"Well," I said, "that's your idea, but it isn't mine."

"Well, if you believe in that so strong, why don't you get out here and stand up and say, 'They can't hit me—I pray, they can't hit me!'"

I kind of looked at him. I said, "Well, you got things all wrong. The good Lord gave me sixteen weeks of Basic in Camp Wolters, Texas. They taught me how to take care of myself when I'm in combat. Now if I don't use those brains they give me, I could stand out there and get nailed right away. I've got to use the knowledge that I got to protect myself. There's no doggone way the Kraut over here are going to get me because I'm going home when this thing is

1944 – "All who were able moved forward." (History of the 120th Infantry Regiment)

over."

He just kind of took that with a grain of salt.

Then shells kept coming in, and all of a sudden one come just zoom, boom, and just broke the dirt in our hole—cracked it. Then we heard a tick . . .

Well, it'll tick just a few seconds, and then it blows. That's those delayed actions. When they're ticking, they're live. There's no doubt about it. This, of course, happened in just a matter of seconds.

He poked me and said, "Albrecht, you prayin'?"

I said, "You bet I'm prayin'!"

He poked me again. "Are you prayin' for me?"

"Ya, I'm prayin' for you."

He said, "Pray out loud—I want to hear my name."

So I did . . . and just like that the ticking stopped. The shell never blew!

He kind of looked—and then said, "You know, when I get home, I'm going to be religious."

"Well," I said, "I don't think I'd wait that long. You better start right now and start believing—then you got a chance to get home."

I don't know if the guy made it home—I'm sure he did. Something happened so that we got separated, so I never did see him again.

***

September 25, 1944: "One of the big items of news here at home is the all-time record of food production that has been achieved by American farmers. American industry has been setting all kinds of records in this war, and you probably have heard a lot about the mountains of tanks, planes, ships and other weapons that have been turned out. But you ought to know something too, about the mountains of food which American farms have produced since Pearl Harbor—a greater supply than any nation at war has ever had at its disposal . . ."

"Farms," *Life*, Special issue, A Letter to GIs, September 25, 1944.

Private Albrecht:
POTATOES

Everyone was harping about potatoes—"Gee, would that ever be good . . ."

We had a fire going in this house and that night we were chewin' the fat. Here comes a shell in close to the house, and I thought, "Boy, we should get the hell out of here!"

But in the morning, here was a hole in front of the steps where the shell came in—some of our windows were broken. We looked and saw humps all over the place. Here it was potatoes! All we had to do was rub off the dirt and we had potatoes!

You see, they had pulled all the vines so you couldn't tell that anything was planted—then after the war, they would have their potatoes.

Travel Day 4:
Grown-Up Towns

I WONDER IF DAD REALLY DID EXPECT to see Camp Chicago. That's where, after the war had ended, he waited out his orders to ship home. Naturally his memories were fond, about relaxation and good eats, "just waiting to go home." I tell this out of sequence in his stories because Reims is the city we were heading to next, and we hoped that just maybe we would run into this Camp Chicago. Dad remembered that it was "right out of Reims." More on this later, but this illustrates our method of operation.

We were off again on the hunt, focused mostly this day on getting through France and on toward Belgium. Dad got us up by seven o'clock, and as an unfortunate repeat of the previous day, no options for breakfast were available at or near the hotel. We took off on the road around Paris headed to Reims with an eye for any sign of a restaurant along the way. Again, it was late in the morning before that happened.

Our collective attitudes could have been described as less than chipper, definitely not upbeat. The couple of encounters with haughty Frenchmen the day before somehow had clouded our overall view of the place, enough to question even the whole point of our trip. Well, not in so many words, but Wilt and I for sure wondered just what we had gotten ourselves—and Dad—into. What if the trip was a bust? How much could we hope to accomplish? You just shouldn't take an aging parent looking for old memories on a road trip without backup. And so much for my expectations of that perfect trip. As for Dad, he was unusually quiet except for a grumble now and then about not seeing any signs for a restaurant. Honestly, a cup of coffee could have made the difference those first hours on the road.

But the mood brightened with the day, sunnier than recent days and slightly warmer. And a stop at a gas station brought comic relief as well as a take-out coffee. Dad was busy looking through postcards to send back home to my sisters and to the employees where he worked at the gas station. I heard him chuckle. "Hey, you two, look at this one," he said as he headed to the cashier with the cards. The French sure have a way about them, if you know what I mean . . ."

We looked. Then I gasped. "Gee, Dad, isn't this . . . well . . . too risqué? I mean, especially for a *postcard* . . . just out there for the Morgan mailman to see, too . . . ?" The cartoon couldn't have been more explicit with women's body parts, with something written in French at the bottom.

"No, no, no. This is a really *good* one for the guys at the station." Dad beamed as he set the cards on the counter, the sexy one on top so the clerk was sure to take note. "They think I'm half dead anyway. I don't know what the heck it says, but it will give them something to talk about." He continued to chuckle under his breath, amused with his clever find.

The clerk didn't appear to understand English, but she seemed intrigued enough in this old guy and his purchase to give us a grin and a wink.

That stop got us over the slump, on to a café, and into Reims with renewed energy for whatever lay ahead on this history hunt. Europe was ours again—well, maybe not this larger-than-expected city of Reims. As we entered the thickening traffic on the outskirts of town, we rethought our objectives. These cities were daunting enough just to get around. Camp Chicago, we decided, likely was long gone—after all, wasn't it a temporary American facility during the war? Dad wasn't sure.

Good thing we didn't veer off course in search of Camp Chicago. I've learned now that it was one of nineteen re-deployment camps around Reims. "Tent camp" is what they were called, all named after American cities. Though temporary to suit the specific purpose of war, these camps offered the soldiers a home base while awaiting their shipping orders. For Dad at least, Camp Chicago would continue to exist through his 1944 snapshots and stories.

Though giving up on finding the actual camp, we did drive toward the center of town looking for landmarks that perhaps Dad remembered when he had day passes from the camp. There we found the famous Gothic architectural landmark of France, the Cathedral Notre Dame de Reims. This Dad remembered. In 1944-1945, the cathedral, still scarred from World War I, was sand-bagged to twenty feet on all sides by the Americans. He told us too that it was Reims where the Germans surrendered unconditionally to the Allies ending the fighting in Europe. That was on May 7, 1945. And here we stood again with a full dose of history.

But, our travel clock told us to get on the move. Bastogne was where we wanted to get by mid-afternoon. Our eagerness to get out of France did seem a bit hasty, now that we were just getting an appreciation for the French flair. Strolling the streets and grabbing fresh fruit in France's renowned champagne region, where coronations were held for French kings, where world peace was accorded—well, that could be a trip in itself. Perhaps this was how we should leave France, with a desire one day to come back.

The two-and-a-half-hour drive to Bastogne focused us on the Battle of the Bulge, the largest battle fought by the Americans in World War II. During the winter months of 1944-1945, this was the Nazi's last ditch effort against the Allies. The Ardennes Offensive as it was known became more commonly called the Battle of the Bulge because the initial attack by the Germans created a bulge in the Allied front line. It was on this front line where Dad spent six days and nights in a foxhole on a hill overlooking the Germans. The hill was what we intended to find.

Coming from the south as we were, first would be Bastogne, the center of the battle, there along Belgium's hilly border with Luxembourg. Then some forty miles northeast into Belgium would be the smaller city of Malmedy . . . and, hopefully, the hill. Being so focused on Malmedy and that hill, we almost neglected to take a good look at Bastogne. Thankfully, we did.

Quaint and charming with its shops and restaurants, modern-day Bastogne also speaks boldly in honor of the American troops who fought in the battle that claimed 19,000 dead, 47,500 wounded, 23,000 missing. Though most of the population in Bastogne are French-speaking, English now is a close second. A U.S. Sherman tank is displayed in the town center, along with a statute of the U.S. Commander McAuliffe. His famous "Nuts!" response to the German commander's demand for surrender was heard around the world.

An exhibition hall depicts numerous lifelike dioramas from the war, and at the outskirts of town is the stately Mardasson Memorial towering in the design of the five-pointed American star. The Latin inscription on the memorial stone translates to "The Belgium people remember their American liberators." This is Tribute.

Our photo of Dad standing next to the Sherman tank is my favorite from that day. He is smiling, the sun is shining. Finally, he is in his element—this is what he came to see. "Boy, oh boy . . ." he reminded us as we got back in our car, "that McAuliffe really told those Germans, didn't he? They didn't know what they were up against with us Americans. That's for darned sure."

1992 – Mardasson Memorial in the design of the five-pointed American star, Bastogne, Belgium. (Author's Collection)

1992 – Dad in Bastogne, Belgium, at the display of a U.S. Sherman tank. (Author's Collection)

Heading out of town now, we could feel a momentum building. Maybe we were just getting into the rhythm of this car-trip-across-Europe travel—no matter, the three of us shuffling around in all this history was invigorating. Perhaps we were settling into the ups and downs of our journey. Just maybe, I'd get that perfect trip.

The lateness in the day and the idea that we might find cheaper accommodations veered us off our main road into Luxembourg. Just fifteen miles from Bastogne we found the pretty little town of Clervaux, absolutely a welcome sight after navigating Paris and Reims just that morning.

Clervaux Castle is situated in the middle of town on a rocky spur surrounded on three sides by a loop in the River Clerve—it commands attention. This twelfth-century castle with its history of counts and lords was badly damaged in the Battle of the Bulge. Since restored, the castle now houses a museum from the battle, as well as offices of the local government and a gallery of Alfred Steichen photographs.

Looking up at this castle as we slowly made our way into this mystical town nestled in the Ardennes, we couldn't help but imagine a movie set. Drama was everywhere with the forest, the river, the rocky slopes, the castle, the quaint buildings—the tightness of everything in this valley. Our earlier concern for economy was quickly out the window with an urge to experience this unique stop no matter the cost. Our dinner at Hotel des Nations was fitting for royalty—wild boar for the gents, trout for madame. And the down comforters at Auberge des Ardennes were nothing less than heavenly. Perfect.

***

November 1944: "The mud, rain, and cold added to the miseries of war, but all of this could have been endured with little thought if there had been any reason to believe that the enemy was whipped. But this he certainly was not. More than one veteran, as he lay in a basement or sweated it out in a foxhole, wondered how much farther his luck would carry him. It was without question a depressing period for our troops. The only way out was to attack, to move forward, to drive even deeper into the unknown fortress of Germany."

November 1944, *History of the 120th Infantry Regiment*,
by Officers of the Regiment (Infantry Journal Press, 1947).

Private Albrecht:
THOSE LUCKY TANKERS

We took another town, and the infantry guys, I suppose me included, were all kind of complaining that, okay, we take a town, and then when we get it secured, the tanks come up and act as mobile artillery. That isn't the way we were taught in basic. Down there they said, "The tanks go first and get any big stuff, and then you guys come and mop up." But it was just the opposite.

So we were squawking, and finally our officers and tank commander met. The guy in the tanks said, "Okay, we've got five light tanks for your outfit here, and we're not going to go ahead of you, and we won't go behind you. We'll go right with you. When your men are going across the fields to attack, we'll go right with you. But we want four infantry men on top of each tank."

There would be four men in the tank, and then there would be four of us on top of the tank. So that was twenty men we had to have to go on the tanks, and I got picked as one of 'em.

The four of us sat on top of the tank, and when we would get into a town and come to a crossroad, it was our duty to jump off and take a look and see if there was any heavy stuff down on the streets. If there wasn't, we would wave our tank through, hop back on and go a little farther. Then if we spotted a group, we'd tap down, and they would notify the gunner and he'd let 'em have it. That first day we took that town, and it worked real good.

It had rained a lot, you know, and there were a lot of beets planted. You walked through those fields, and you'd slip on your fanny most of the time because it was so doggone slippery. So here we were riding! Gee, that was nice. Then at night we would stay in the basement with those tankers instead of in a foxhole. They also had ten-in-one rations which was like a banquet to us.

The next day then we took another town—or were supposed to take it. We got halfway over, and a few balls of fire come tearing across the sky. The five tanks stopped. I was on the middle tank, the third tank, which was the commander's tank. We stopped, and they opened the hatch and looked around. I said, "What happens if we meet a Tiger Royal up in the next town?" Tiger Royal was the biggest German tank—it had an eighty-eight-millimeter gun on it. Our tanks had thirty-seven millimeter—that was like a pea-shooter compared to them.

"Don't worry," he said, "if we see a Tiger Royal, we're going to turn around and get the hell out of there!"

Okay. Pretty soon we started, and we got near the end of town. There was a hedge down at the end of the town, and our five tanks would come through in a row back there. There was a sunken road there by that hedge, and here was a Tiger Royal sitting down in there with the muzzle sticking through that hedge a little bit, which nobody saw until all of a sudden . . . whoom, and the first tank blew all to smithereens! The four guys on it flew in all directions. It burned right away, and whoom, the second one got it and the same thing there—guys all flew in pieces! I was just gettin' ready to jump off of ours—all of us were—and then ours got hit!

By that time, the other two tanks had turned and were getting back to safety. Ours got hit, and well, Clarence Dale was sitting next to me—just in that split second, I don't know how you can explain it any other way, but we were practically touching each other, and I saw part of his neck and his left shoulder and arm all gone—just that quick. Red Degenhardt was ahead of me, and I could see he was done for. The other guy up in the front, he seemed to be okay. We all flew off through the air.

I picked myself up, and I got in back of our tank—ours wasn't burning— and this other kid from New York got back there with me. We were the only two live ones out of twenty-four men on those three tanks!

Then as we stood behind our tank, this Tiger Royal shot a phosphor shell at our tank. That caught it on fire, and it came in the front end and some out the *back, and a chunk of the shrapnel caught me in the hip. There I had that chunk sticking out! I had a jacket on and cartridge belt and pants belt and all that . . . and that's where the shrapnel went. It stuck out about four inches—it burned because of the phosphorous.*

This kid from New York said, "Hey, you're hit!"

"Ya, but it can't be too bad."

There was a German foxhole over there a ways, so we decided we would make a run for it. We did and dove into there. Got down, and pretty soon, the kid, he looked up and said, "Gol, dang, Albrecht, we're the only two up here. There isn't anybody else up here!"

There were barbed wire entanglements between us and the safety back there. We had gone over them with the tank, and then they bounced right back up. He said, "Well, you think you can make it? You think we can run for it?"

There was a wall back there which we wanted to get behind—a stone wall. I said, "Well, I'll try it."

So out of the hole. We come up to this entanglement barbed wire deal, and he made a jump and made it through. I jumped, and I got right in the middle of it because I couldn't jump too good with that chunk in my hip. I kind of hung there in the barbed wire. All of a sudden whoosh the old shell came by. I know he wasn't shooting at me, but he must have been shooting at something right in line, and my helmet flew off and everything. I don't know how I got my feet out, but I sure got out of that barbed wire!

I got back of that wall, and our medic, he was busier than Sam Hill, you know, with guys laying around—most of them dead, of course, from the tanks, but some other ones getting hit too. The lieutenant saw I could walk, and he said, "Say that farm place we come through just about a quarter of a mile back through the field—some doctors moved into there and some MPs. You think you could make it back there?"

"Well, I'll sure try."

He said, "Go ahead." So I started to walk, and I got near the edge where the field was to start out across, and another American officer, he let out a beller, "Hey! You stop damm it, or I'll let you have it!" He had the rifle on me.

I thought, "Well, what in the Sam Hill's the matter with you?"

He come up and said, "You're not sneaking out of here—get back up there!"

I said, "I'm not sneaking out. That's my orders. I'm supposed to go and have this tended."

He looked. "Oh, oh, I'm sorry—I didn't know you were hit. That's okay . . . Say . . . how about taking three prisoners with you?"

"Okay."

So he brought three Heinies over there—blonds, big guys. I got them ahead of me, and I told them, "Mach schnell, hurry up, and keep your hands up and stay apart!"

We didn't get very far and the big one in the middle, he said something in German which I couldn't understand, and then they all got together.

I thought, "Oh, oh, they're going to try something on me here"—me a single guy. I could remember every shell I shot out of my rifle, and I knew I only had one shell left in the clip, and there were three guys there. That didn't pan out so good. I had the bayonet on, and I hollered to them again to get apart, you know, you get rough with them. They got apart but just for a little ways, and pretty soon that big blond in the middle, he was giving them orders again or something, and they got together again. This time I just ran up ahead with the bayonet on there, and I left a pretty good scar in that big one's butt, and from then on I had no problem. They stayed apart! We got in to that farm place, and I turned them over to the MPs.

Then I went in where the medics were, and they got me on the table. I took down my britches, and they told me, "Don't touch that—let the doctor do that." He pulled that out and then got some stuff and doped it up, powder and stuff that they put on to keep the infection out. He put some bandages on and was gettin' ready to get a tag and get my name and so forth. About that time a couple of stretchers came in with two guys on, and they were bloody from head to foot. In fact, they looked like they were dead, but the medic he said, "Oh, I got to give them plasma. I'll be back in a little bit."

Well, he started working on them, and I thought to myself, "Holy buckets, they are really hurt—what the heck am I doing here taking up a medic's time when I can walk?' So I got off the table and got my britches up and looked outside. There was a major just going to get into a Jeep. So I went out the door and went over to him. I said, "Where are you heading?"

"Well," he said, "I'm going up to the town. It's secure now."

I said, "Well I'll go along with you." So I hopped in.

Well, you see the doctors didn't have my name, not a doggone thing so there was no record on that particular time that I'd been hit. That's the record that I finally got after the war was over, when I saw that you got ten points for it. One reason I didn't want them—I knew if they got my name, they would send my wife a telegram that I'd been hit, and I didn't want that. I said I would write to her and let her know. So I just didn't pay any more attention until of course the war was over.

I had to stay with the lieutenant down in the CP, and I let our medic handle it down there. I told him, "Oh, heck, Doc, you can handle it."

"Gol dang," he said, "you're getting too big a job on my hands."

I said, "You do a good job." Well then I had to stay down and tend to the phone in the CP. It turned out that I was there, I suppose, with the lieutenant about, oh, two weeks, something like that.

***

1944-1945: Cartoonist Dave Breger first coined "G.I. Joe"—derived from the term Government Issue—in his 1942 cartoon strip for *Yank*. The name was in wide use by the end of the war and so synonymous with the everyman soldier that a 1945 movie celebrating the common infantryman, based on war correspondent Ernie Pyle's columns was called "The Story of G.I. Joe".   *World War II*, May/June 2012

Private Albrecht:
HELPING OUT

    I had to stay with the lieutenant at the Command Post for about two weeks after I was hit with the shrapnel. One night the phone rang, and I answered it. It was 12:30 to 1:00 at night and the 119th Regiment was supposed to take the next town. The big commander couldn't get any information. They lost all track of it, and he didn't know if they took the town, or if they were captured, or what the heck. He was calling our lieutenant to see if he couldn't send somebody over to that town to see if the Germans had it or if we had it. Well, the lieutenant says, "Heck, that isn't ours—we are the 120th—that's nothing to do with us."

    "Ya, but that doesn't make any difference. You're Thirtieth and we haven't any information, and we want to have it."

    "Well, okay," he said, "we're going to have to wake somebody up."

    The lieutenant said he'd go. He said, "I'm not going to pick a guy out to do that all by himself. I'll go, but I should have some fire power."

    "Well," I said, "heck, I'll put some bandoliers around my neck"—because I couldn't wear them around my belt yet or anything like that, pants belt or any of that, "and I'll go along and give you fire power."

    You know . . . you volunteer for stuff that now you'd think you had rocks in your head. But I did, and so he and I took off on this darned old road for that town. We got fairly close to it, and there was a wheat stack, or whatever it was, out there someplace burning that gave a little light. We got near the town, and nobody stopped us . . . we couldn't figure what the heck. We stayed probably fifteen yards apart, but then every once in a while we'd get together, and the lieutenant said, "Gol darn, I don't like this . . ."

That didn't sound good. We got a little closer, and pretty soon we saw a bunch of American Jeeps all lined up along one of the buildings. "Oh, oh," he said, "now I really don't like it. Nobody's out here to stop us!" You see, they would have this all posted.

We came by a building, and I could see right down near the sidewalk there was like a basement window. It was blacked out, but I could see a crack of light there. So I kind of got down, and I listened, and, gol dang, it was all German! I thought, "Oh, oh."

So I beat it up and got the lieutenant, and I said, "Come on back here and listen."

He came back. It was all German talkin'. "Well," he said, "then the Germans have got it. That's, I suppose, about it."

Well, we walked up a little farther. There were two buildings that were a ways apart but they had a wall right along the sidewalk, just a gateway, and then kind of a yard in there. We got just about there, and the shells came in. So we had no choice but to go in there quick. The way they were coming in, we just went up to the door of that building where we heard the Germans talking, and we barged right on in. We were in a hallway when we got in the door, and down at the end of the hallway there was a little light under one of the doors. Down there we went, and the lieutenant says, "Well, here goes, Albrecht!" He just kind of batted open the door.

Here was a bunch of American officers around the table! They looked at us like—"What the Sam Hill's the matter with you guys?"

Then the lieutenant started chewin' them out. Here they thought they had all the guards out, outposts all around, everything protected. They had taken the town, and the prisoners were in the basement. That's why we heard all that German. They herded them all down the basement and just kept 'em down there.

After the lieutenant got done chewin' them out and everything, well, then he and I headed back across that doggone old road again—burnt-out tanks, trucks and stuff along the way—and back to our guys. We told 'em, "Now when you see a couple guys coming back tonight, don't get trigger happy!" because our guys would be out in their holes watching. If somebody is coming down the road, you know, you're apt to get shot. We got back okay.

The next night the intelligence notified us that the Germans were going to come in that night with a tank or two—not the same road, but a crossroad there, a tar road—they were going to be coming in. We didn't have anything to stop them outside of road mines. We didn't know for sure just exactly what to do about that. Then they decided we would take some mines, big ones, out by this crossroad and tie ropes on them and leave them on like a shoulder or a little edge off, and then lay on the opposite side of the road. Then, when the tanks would come, they wouldn't see anything on the road. And when they'd get up there, then we'd yank that old mine out so they'd run over it and blow the tank up. Well, that didn't sound too appetizing, but that's what we did.

Just luckily, no tanks came that night. They had screwed up, so we didn't have to do that.

All in all, that time I spent in the Command Post with that lieutenant was anything but good. It was a rough spot because we did a lot of stuff. Then you volunteer for all that dang junk yet.

***

November 7, 1944: Franklin Roosevelt is elected to a fourth term in office. He remains the only president to have served more than two terms.   www.history.com

Private Albrecht:
SMALL TARGET

Size in the Army doesn't mean much normally. I mean, you know in civilian life, why if you are a big bruiser, everybody better behave or you clobber them or whatever. If you're not too big and so forth, you might say you are handicapped a little bit.

In the Army, the little guy is probably the best off of all them. You're a lot smaller target, and you have that rifle in your hands. It doesn't make any difference if you're four feet tall or you're eight feet tall, when you've got that rifle, you do the same damage, only you're a smaller target. That's one way you're even and, I don't know, you do things that normally you wouldn't ever think of doing. You've got that rifle in your hand, and you're not worried, you're not scared. You'd think all the time the stuff you go through that you'd be so doggoned scared you'd be shaking all over, but that isn't the case. You're not scared.

In fact, we had a number of fellows . . . well, if you watched Patton, *when he visited a hospital, he came to this one guy and he asked the doctor, "What's the matter with him?"*

"Oh, it's kind of a nervous breakdown."

And you know what Patton said—"Get that SOB out of here, and get him out now, or I'll kick him out!" Oh, he called him everything he could think of. You know, coward and everything else. That's just the way he was.

Some guys will really shake, I mean, I don't know what makes the difference. I know a lot of times I would even try and shake to see how I could do that, but I couldn't even fake it. There was no way I could do it so that it would look real. You pretty near had a notion to try it once in a while, you know, to get out of there.

I had one guy in a hole, I didn't even know him yet—he got in the hole at just about dark, and a German plane came over and dropped a flare. Of course, that lights everything up like day. Then the plane dropped a bomb, and it looked

like it was coming right for our hole. It usually does when you look up, but heck that missed us by probably a block or half a block, and he wasn't aiming at us anyway, I'm sure. That guy with me, he just shrank over in the corner and just stared. He didn't blink his eyes—that was it. Then the next morning, they came and hauled him out. He couldn't talk—nothing. It just scared him so bad that he couldn't move, that's all.

One time we were in the field and had to just stop and lie there. You lay there and saw the dirt fly around you, and, boy, if you could be smaller yet, you sure would, I'll guarantee you that. You feel awfully big about that time.

No, you have no objection to being small when you're in there, that's for doggone sure.

Travel Day 5 (Part I):
900 Yards of Flat Land

RESTED AND GEARED UP FOR OUR SEARCH mission again, we left comfortable little Luxembourg where the pressure to find things was laid aside that one night. Travel just for the sake of travel. A look at the map again convinced us to hold off on Malmedy one more day for efficiency's sake. We could catch it easily then on our way to Nuremberg.

Instead, we headed north to the Aachen area of Germany, an area of major conflict in the fall of 1944 where Germany, Belgium, and the Netherlands all come together. Aachen, there on Germany's western border, had been incorporated into the impressive German defensive network, known as the Siegfried Line, a devilish mix of entanglements, fortifications, and tank traps. But despite this formidable barrier, Aachen would be the first city on German soil to be captured by the Allies.

"Northeast of Aachen" is where Dad recounted "holding high ground" in anticipation of the next objective, Hitler's SS troops, his elite, in the nearby town of Euchen. This is specifically where we were headed, though in this densely populated area, no where did we see Euchen on our map. We relied on Dad's memory and whatever details we could piece together from *History of the 120th Infantry Regiment*. Easy enough, we thought back home, but now standing on solid ground in this grown-up area of one city running into another, Wilt and I secretly worried that we could just as well come up empty handed. We stole glances at each other, rolling our eyes. Dad's unflinching gaze, on the other hand, was out the window watching for any clue of 1944 Euchen.

It seems to me that many of the difficulties of foreign travel stem simply from mispronunciation. In Mexico for instance, where Wilt and I have traveled frequently, we continue to marvel at the quizzical looks we get whenever our enunciation is just the slightest bit off, as though the word is no where to be found in the Spanish language. Likely it's our lazy English habits. Even the word "margarita" if not crisp with the r and the i, can bring a questioning look. Now here in Germany, the "Euchen (You-chen)" version that we spilled out in our exasperated stops to ask for directions, map in hand stabbing in the general area northeast of Aachen, lead only to blank shrugs. And after several of these shrugs, our shoulders also took on the same motion and, worse, eventually dropped to a slouch. We pulled out of the traffic into a gas station parking lot to regroup and consider a Plan B for the day.

But a kindly gas station attendant—I'll call him "attendant guy"—came to our rescue noticing us in the parked car with map spread across the dash. He knocked on Dad's window and hollered, "*Guten Morgen!*"

We turned from the map to see his smiling face up close to the window, and Dad hurriedly rolled it down. "You bet! *Guten Morgen* to you!" Dad responded so joyfully that if ever this attendant guy had even a minor dislike for Americans, that opinion would be forever changed. The two men, two different languages, obviously spoke the same social values.

Reacting as if without even a second to spare, we three automatically pointed to our map and asked, "Euchen?" in high voices. Accustomed now to the language barrier, we each dramatized our dilemma with accentuated furrowed brows and shrugged shoulders. Without a common language, certainly we could act it out.

"*Nein, nein . . .*" was all he said slowly shaking his head, even as we repeated the name even louder. Grabbing the map, Wilt shoved it in front of attendant guy and pointed out Aachen and the general vicinity. I grabbed a notepad, scribbled out "Euchen," and put that in front of him too. Attendant guy's eyes lit up as he saw the word spelled out. "Euchen (Ouy-chen)!" he blurted as if solving a puzzle. "Euchen!" He emphasized the "ouy" sound, and now we were speaking the same language. With excitement even to match ours, attendant guy pointed to a precise spot on our map near Aachen, the Nordrhein-Westfalen area, just where we suspected though not marked, and he pointed out a route for us as well. "Euchen!" he repeated like a teacher. The three of us said it in unison, he nodded approval, and we all laughed. Then for good measure, we said it again and giggled with relief.

Glad at least to know the German words for thank you, we gushed that out, and we each shook his hand. "*Danke, danke, danke.*" We waved and drove off uplifted, knowing that despite language miscues, people *do* connect. The four of us were somehow better for the experience. For all of you attendant guys out there in the world, thank you.

Now, the business of not only finding the town but also the "900 yards of flat land" coming into town—that's how Dad described the area where troops were ordered to walk in broad daylight to overtake the SS troops on November 16, 1944. This scene was "the perfect attack" as it is described in *The History of the 120th Infantry Regiment*.

Attendant guy's directions were perfect. We drove the side roads of Euchen and circled as best we could. It's true, just as Dad had described, there were woods on one end of town and then this open area on the other, now with fences and planted crops. Where we sensed might be the army's approach, we turned off to follow a farming road up close to the city limits.

That's when Wilt abruptly stopped the car and got out—a dip in the terrain struck a chord. Could this be the sunken railroad tracks that Dad described? He and I got out too, and the three of us walked this sunken spot. We poked with sticks into the weeds and overgrowth. Nothing. "Well, I sure remember tumbling down something like this when I came upon those surprised Germans." Dad was surveying the mounded earth on the sides. "Yup, this could be the place all right." He stood back and eyed the mound and then the short distance to the edge of town. "Uh, hah . . ."

Wilt and I continued to poke the weeds, glad that at least Dad seemed satisfied. But were *our* expectations set too high to verify the details some forty-eight years later? In a field? For all practical purposes, we had located the town and general area of the attack, which in this case had to be good enough, right? We poked more at the ground.

"Come on, you two, how about we head into the town and see what's there?" Dad was on his way to the car. Reluctant to end our search, we walked back slowly, eyes still focused on the ground. That's when persistence paid off: Wilt spotted it—there sticking out from the asphalt was a piece of railroad track. Apparently, at some point the track was removed except for under a road such as this. For us, that common sense of the railway boss preserved a valuable clue. Affirmation! Thank you, God! All of our set-backs and frustrations, even those still ahead, were worth this piece of track. Dad bent down at the edge of the road and ran his fingers over the track, and we waited for him to make the final call. When he looked at us, he was beaming. "Well, I'll be darned," was all he could say.

With energy to spare, now convinced one hundred percent that we had found the site, we hurried back to the main road and followed it into the center of town. The afternoon offered plenty of time to scout out the town for more findings. From our vantage point out on that field, we had spotted a couple of steeples, and that was the side of town where we were headed. A bell tower was where Dad had suspected a sniper's shot came from that killed his captain standing next to him that day after the troops had taken the town. It was at that bell tower that Dad made his "first aimed shot," as he always described it . . . in a sanitized sort of way. "Shooting from the hip" was the other sort of combat he described, not an aim on a particular soldier, just wide-range of shots at whatever was ahead. But we kids heard the story of the aimed shot many times growing up and never once questioned the motive of that shot or, for that matter, any of the aimed shots he would be taking those long months on the front lines. We were mesmerized with the action of U.S. Army versus the enemy. And he was our dad. He had a plan to get back home alive.

Winding our way through the town's busy, narrow streets, we finally found the town center. Two bell towers within a couple of blocks of each other seemed to fit Dad's description so we stopped and took photos of both. The bustling street scene seemed to stand still as we stood looking up at the steeples, imagining the scene from 1944: Allied troops overtaking the city, snipers holding on to a last grasp, a soldier reacting to even the score with a German in a bell tower. The moment turned solemn.

Finally, I spoke up, "Well, okay, what do you think—should we check out those churches and find out more about them? I'll bet we can find someone who knows the history."

"No, no, no, that's okay, Faye." Dad was quick to answer. "These two churches look old enough, and that's good enough for me. Besides, I see a little café across the street that looks pretty good about now."

We were ready to move on.

1992 – Possibly the steeple from 1944 in Euchen, Germany. (Author's Collection)

***

November 1944: "The entire lst Battalion had been assembled in the courtyard of the rest area 'monastery' at Kerkrade several days prior to the attack to hear an orientation talk delivered by Major Williamson, battalion commander."

History of the 120th Infantry Regiment, by Officers of the
Regiment (Infantry Journal Press 1947)

Private Albrecht:
REST BEFORE THE ATTACK

We were holding high ground northeast of Aachen, and we knew that sooner or later we were going to have to take the town of Euchen. That wasn't going to be an easy job because there were all SS troops in there—that's Hitler's elite troops. We were all thinking about that . . . with a couple of live pillboxes out there where we were going to have to go across.

Then all of a sudden we were told, "There's some troops going to be moving in here. They're going to occupy your holes, and you're going back for a rest."

Wow, of course, that sounded extra good the first time. I thought, "Gee, that's very nice of them . . ."

Here comes a whole bunch of troops marching up the road. They hadn't been in combat or nothing. That day some of us were in the barn, and when the guys started coming by, we said, "Come on, come on, get in the barn, get in the barn!"

They looked at us and didn't know what to do. Their officer was marching them, and finally we yelled again, "Hey, you guys—gol dang it, get apart! Come on get in here!"

Well, a couple of them did. Then the officers started chewing them out. See, they weren't supposed to do that.

We said, "Come on, or you're going to get nailed!"

The doggone officer still kept part of them guys marching down, and all of a sudden the shells came in like we knew they would, because that was every day. A whole bunch of them got hit just for his stupidness. That's all it was.

Well anyway, they occupied our holes, and then we walked back about, oh, a half to three-quarters of a mile, and then a truck picked us up and took us in to this monastery near Spekholzerheide. It was a real big building, long, like "L" shaped, right by a little river—lots of religious shrines and stuff in there with these monks, whatever. But everybody had a little stall with a cot in and a sink, no toilet. There were three floors, and it held a heck of a bunch of men. I don't know how many, but everybody had a bed.

There was a big room that they used for a dining room where you could eat sort of cafeteria style getting your grub. The Thirtieth Division Orchestra was there and played for breakfast, dinner, and supper each day that you were there— the two days.

You didn't answer to anybody—you were as free as a bird. And we weren't even back as far as our heavy artillery! That was still farther back, and boy, we felt like we were practically in heaven. They had the windows all blocked off and had some little fifteen-watt bulb lights in there at night so you could write some letters or stuff, you know.

And they had very good food—that is, good for the Army. They had pretty good cooks. They were using all this dehydrated stuff, but they at least knew how to fix it. That's the first we saw of those little boxes you know, individual boxes of Kellogg's Corn Flakes. I'll never forget that first morning we came in there for breakfast, and I saw those. And it sounds like I'm lying, but I know I ate six or seven boxes of them Corn Flakes! You could have all you wanted, no limit. For dinner we'd make two or three trips—supper we'd make a couple of trips, you know. We ate . . . oh, my gosh!

Well, then the second day everybody had the runs! I think your stomach wasn't used to, you know, getting full. They checked the kitchen to see if there wasn't something wrong there. They couldn't find anything. Then each floor had a lister bag—that's what your water is in, a great big canvas bag on a tripod and then some faucets on it, and that's all Army water—nothing else to drink. They started checking those to see if maybe something got in one. Well, the one up on the third floor had an old dirty sock in it, but that's the only thing they could find, but that wouldn't affect all the rest of them, so that wasn't the problem.

The way it was outside over this creek—they'd built just like a bridge, you know, and then they had boards on there like seats and a rest for your back, and that was your toilet. You go and sit on that, and it would go right down in the creek so you didn't need to flush anything. Boy, I tell you that night it was pitch dark, and I woke up—I had cramps. A lot of the guys didn't make it—just a little way from their bed, that's as far as they got—some of them on the stairs, some of them hanging their butt out of the window, and the floors. It was one heck of a mess, I guarantee you. But what are you going to do about it?

Anyway, I made it down, and I thought, "Golly, I wonder if I can find that place in the dark out there at that creek." Well, all you had to do was put your hand out in front of you and you were touching somebody's shoulder, so it was no problem—you were right there and waited your turn on that bridge. I don't know, they probably had a place for twenty-five guys to sit there at once if you wanted to, you know. They were full.

That's the way it turned out. I think it was the food—nothing bad—it was just that your system wasn't used to that because, oh, boy, did we shove it in.

But then we found out the reason for this rest. Whenever you were going to make a big attack—and they had things pretty well planned out—they wanted you rested up for that. They sent us back like that for a rest, and then when we came back, those other troops got out of there that were occupying our holes. Then it was just a matter of a day or two and then we made the attack on Euchen.

***

November 16, 1944: "The advance was made according to a field manual writer's dream as a constant stream of fire was placed on the enemy's strongpoint in Euchen while the infantry was attacking. When our forces reached the railroad embankment, the artillery fire lifted, and there our men were, looking right down the throats of the Germans . . . Coordination was the explanation for the success of the attack. In turn, this coordination was in large measure the result of days of planning by the Regimental commander and subordinate leaders."

History of the 120th Infantry Regiment, by Officers of the
Regiment (Infantry Journal Press, 1947)

Private Albrecht:
THE PERFECT ATTACK

The location of our attack was a bare 900 yards of flat land. There were no bushes, no nothing outside of two pillboxes that were live, I mean operated by Germans. That was in the Siegfried Line.

We had to go through there, and on one end of the town of Euchen there were woods coming up to it. Naturally, that would be the place where you would come in to attack the town. You wouldn't come out over the open area.

1944 – "Lieutenant Colonel Contey described his battalion's part of 'The Perfect Infantry Attack' to General Simpson and other senior officers of the Ninth Army." (History of the 120th Infantry Regiment)

We were shelling continually back and forth all the time. All of a sudden we got orders to line up in a long line in this open area with the pillboxes out there—and on a beautiful day, no clouds, nice and clear, sunshine. They said, "At twelve o'clock we'll blow the whistle, and when we blow the whistle, you start walking for the town of Euchen. You don't run and don't go slow, just a good walk. The reason for that is we're going to be shooting artillery right over your heads, our own, so it'll land out in front of you, and it will blow up any mines that are around there so you don't step in them. That's how we're going to go over, right smack in the middle of the day."

They had a couple of big, like bulldozers, you know, tanks with a blade. They would head for the pillboxes and push dirt up against them and plug up their holes where their guns come out of. Then they put these, what looked like, beehives by the back doors where the guys come out, big iron doors—the beehive was a powerful explosive. They would plant that by the door and light it and get the heck out of the way. That took care of them, what was inside or out. The door came off for sure.

We had grenades hanging out of every pocket and our belts—I was just full of grenades. Our artillery was right over our heads so that we'd walk and all of a sudden you'd be lying there on the ground. You wondered if you were hit or what. You picked yourself up and, by golly, you were all right! It was just the concussion that knocked you down. When we got over to the town of Euchen, I didn't have a grenade left—they flopped off when you got knocked down.

There was a railroad kind of around the town—it was a sunken railroad like their roads. I went down the bank, and I tripped over some barbed wire and I fell. I rolled down there to the tracks but from training, my rifle never got in the dirt. You're awful fussy about that. Here I was on one knee looking at the opposite bank, and I was looking right at three Heinies in a hole! I don't know who was more scared—them or me—but I had the rifle right on them, and boy they got their hands up in a hurry and hollered, "Kamerad, kamerad!"—I shouldn't shoot.

I said, "Kommen ze hier, mach schnell and hands de hop!"
Out they come, and then we didn't have time to frisk them or anything so we just told them to go back where we come from. They didn't want to do that but then we fired a shell or two in the ground right next to them, and then they started moving. We had men back there, you know, MPs and so forth.

Then we got up a little farther, and our captain came by just walking along the line, and he tapped me on the shoulder. "How you doing, Albrecht?"

I said, "Okay."

Just then he got about ten feet from me and he got a bullet right through his neck that took care of him just that quick!

I looked up, and I saw a Heinie hanging out of the church tower up by the bell. He had his gun. I think he was probably the one that got our captain. Anyway, that's the first aimed shot that I took in the service. I shot a lot of times from the hip where you see a bush or something and you blast that, but I never had an aimed one until then. The guy didn't bother any more so I don't know what happened to him, but I just figured maybe somebody else shot the same time I did. Anyway, he didn't bother us, and I went on.

When the captain dropped dead, and I shot up in the church tower, then I just leaned against that building right in the damn middle of it and had to light a cigarette for two or three good puffs to calm my nerves, and then went on.

When we got on the main street, Germans were walking down the street in formation. All the shooting was normal every day. So they didn't think nothing was happening. The officers, when they interviewed them later said, "You guys are nuts to come in the middle of the day and in that open place. You should never have come there. You should have come where the trains were!"

See, they didn't expect anybody from that way. So that took them by surprise, and we got a heck of a bunch of prisoners. In fact, in the Thirtieth Division

book, I believe they call that the most perfect infantry attack of the war—right according to the book. Everything worked just perfect.

1944 – "There wasn't much left of Euchen." (History of the 120th Infantry Regiment)

Travel Day 5 (Part II):
Just Stopping By after Forty-Eight Years

T HE CAFÉ IDEA WAS GOOD. After an already long day with intense study and speculation on attack positions and bell towers with snipers, we needed a break back to the present. Ever mindful that Dad might be fuzzy in any one of his recollections, Wilt and I made sure to proceed with caution each time we set out on a new objective. After all, the last thing we wanted was a big disappointment for Dad on this, a trip of a lifetime. Better put, it was a trip of a past life. Under no circumstances did we want to suggest that perhaps he got the facts all wrong, and we weren't about to say, "Sorry, maybe you just forgot, Dad. Memories sometimes get foggy." That scenario *was not* going to happen.

The piece of railroad track just that morning seemed too good to be true, what with our less-than-systematic approach to this history work. All of this was more of a hit-or-miss approach, working off clues—plus a lot of luck, to be sure, especially in the case of this railroad track. We would savor that find, but, again proceed with caution. Dad at his age might not have the stamina, it was reasonable to assume. So with map in hand, we reviewed again the route of the Thirtieth Division, Dad's stories, and the details of getting from here to there. Faced with the logistics of getting in and around the busy cities, we were well aware now of the obstacles and our limited amount of time.

"Spekholzerheide!" Dad announced boldly as we studied the map of the Aachen area. "That's got to be around here pretty close. That was always the name of the area we had for Bertha." He adjusted his glasses and bent over closer to study the map.

Bertha, long known in our family as the helpful Dutch clerk who assisted Dad in mailing a package back home, was otherwise something of an enigma. When my sisters and I considered our collective memories, Dad's stories didn't include specifics on Bertha. We could only imagine that, even under the most innocent of circumstances, Mom might have been sensitive to the idea of a young Holland woman giving attention—for any reason—to Russ, one of the GIs liberating her homeland. Mom, after all, was the one at home waiting and worrying for two years with her two small girls. Sadly, she exemplified another kind of victim from that war: the spouse left behind. Good reason, Dad probably thought, to leave well enough alone—the acquaintance of Bertha.

But many years of Christmas cards after the war had served to update the Albrecht family and Bertha's. When Bertha married Pierre Urling some years later, that information was shared with the Albrechts, and when the Urlings had a son, Robert, that news too was relayed in their card. As the years passed, they even alluded to Robert's special needs because of a learning disorder. Over the decades, the news became less and less, and then the cards served just as greetings. Eventually, they just stopped.

"That's the heck of it," Dad said, "other than Spekholzerheide, which I don't see here on the map, I only know the name Urling. Pierre Urling, that's her husband."

And that's the information we had when we set out on our new objective: finding Bertha. But again, in the same helpful spirit of the attendant guy that morning, the locals got us pointed in the right direction. Spekholzerheide, we learned, was the part of the Kerkrade community, and that we easily spotted on our map not far from where we were. Dad's sense was right. A check of the community's telephone book brought us to the name "P. Urling, Akerstraat 134, Kerkrade." Could it be that simple? We cautiously wound our way to the address where we found ourselves on a narrow street of brick, three-story row houses.

It was the Urlings' son who answered our knock on the door. Dad stood tall, and his smile was huge. "I'll bet you are Robert? I can recognize you from an old picture."

The young man nodded but with a hesitant look. We weren't anything familiar, not sales people, just foreign-looking strangers.

"Are your mother and dad here?"

Robert nodded and turned, and that's when Bertha joined him at the door, then Pierre. Now there were three wondering about the strangers on their doorstep.

Wilt and I let Dad take the lead. When he said his name, Bertha blinked wide, raised her hands to her face in surprise, and broke into a big, bright smile. She looked at Pierre and said, "This is Russel!"

Pierre, the perfect gentleman, wasted no time to shake Dad's hand and welcome us into the house. "Come in, come in. You are a long way from home." Whether he was the one more fluent in English or was the more outgoing personality, it was he who engaged in most of the conversation as the three of us hobbled together our travel story and why we would show up unannounced. Bertha mostly took it all in quietly. Had we even remotely thought it possible to locate the Urlings, we might have thought wisely to rehearse. As it was, we must have appeared like overly stimulated school children, too excited to complete a thought.

But visiting in their cozy living room and sipping coffee helped us settle in to this new reality: Here was Bertha, the girl from Holland in 1944. Mystery solved, at least part of it. I liked her quiet manner, her gentle eyes. When self-conscious Robert left the room and disappeared upstairs, she looked on lovingly and then returned her attention to us.

Pierre had his own memories of that year, although his were about a time of physical and mental hardship. He was forced by the Germans to leave his family and work in a labor camp. But he remembered jubilation too—joyous

1992 – Dad with his Dutch friend Bertha and Bertha's husband, Pierre, at the Urlings backyard in Spekholzerheide, Netherlands. (Author's Collection)

celebration throughout his homeland when the GIs came to fight for their freedom. "Thank you, Russel," he said more than once.

We couldn't stay long. Now late afternoon, we needed to find a place for the night. Pierre had helped orient us to the town and given us directions for sights the next day: Margraten War Memorial, a place of honor for U.S. soldiers, and, especially for Dad's sake, the location of what might have been the monastery he remembered from 1944. And now when we undoubtedly were looking worn and tired, he phoned a nearby hotel and insisted to lead us in his car. But first, hurried photos in their small backyard, and then we whisked off in our Escort to follow Pierre. Bertha waved at the curb.

Now thinking back, I smile in satisfaction that this other-worldly experience was capped off just right with the stay at this next hotel, The Toucan. Not daring to let on about our penny-pinching mode, with Pierre so helpful, the three of us simply rolled our eyes as we made arrangements with the hotel clerk. All the while, we gawked as inconspicuously as possible at our luxurious surroundings. But once in our rooms, we howled—Pierre certainly did take us to be first-class travelers! We were giddy.

What a day of finds: a battlefield, a person. God's grace.

***

November 13, 1944: "OPA Toyland . . . The 1944 crop of toys is the best since the war. Although there are few metal gadgets, manufacturers have discovered new ways to make playthings out of wood. Most new toys represent a reconversion from war to peace, and a popular item this year is the tractor, instead of last year's Jeep . . ."

Life, November 13, 1944

Private Albrecht:

TWO DOLLS

This Army buddy of mine that was just here to see me a little over a year ago from Pennsylvania—I call him a "buddy," but actually he and I met coming back from the hospital and going back up to the Front. We met in Belgium. He was only twenty and I was thirty-four—I mean he was a lot younger. We were walking down the street, and I came by a store and saw a little doll in the window. I thought, "Gol, darn, I would like to buy that for one of my daughters. I would like two of them—for Mary Jane and Diane."

So we went in, and the few things I had in my pocket to barter with, I didn't have any money—or maybe a little bit but there wasn't much. Anyway, I had enough for one doll but not for two. But this buddy checked over his pocket, and he had just enough for the other one so he was bound and determined I had to take it.

I said, "Well, I don't want to take all your money."

"No," he said, "I don't have anything to spend it for anyway."

So that's the reason I got two dolls to send home—because he divvied up his cash. That was a guy I only knew for two days and wasn't fighting with him or anything. He was in a different outfit—but he's the one that came to see me about a year ago from Pennsylvania, him and his wife.

***

October 1944–May1945: Cohort Profile: The Dutch Hunger Winter Families Study—". . . Despite the war, nutrition in The Netherlands had generally been adequate up to October 1944. Thereafter, food supplies became increasingly scarce. By November 26, 1944, official rations, which eventually consisted of little more than bread and potatoes, had fallen below 1,000 kcal per day, and by April 1945, they were as low as 500 kcal per day. Widespread starvation was seen especially in the cities of the western Netherlands. Food supplies were restored immediately after liberation on May 5, 1945 . . ." L. H. Lumey, et al, "The Dutch Winter Families Study," *International Journal of Epidemiology*, 2007, ije.oxfordjournals.org.

Private Albrecht:
CLEAN HOLLAND

Of all the countries I was in, Holland was the one that really impressed me. I don't know. We came from Belgium and drove into Holland, and you wouldn't need to have a border sign—you could tell just looking at their sparkling windows. It just seemed so clean, and of course, that's the impression I always did have of Holland from a kid on. I always figured that it was a very, very clean place. I agree with that now fully that it is.

In Maastricht, Holland, a buddy and I were walking in town, and we got about halfway down the street when two planes were having a fight up above us. Every store we would go by we would get yanked in. They'd grab a hold of our arm and holler, "Come on, come on. They're fighting up there!"

Hell, we didn't give a damn if they were or not. We were going uptown, and we were used to that, so we just kept on walking.

Finally, one of them came down. We didn't even know if it was ours or the Germans, but it landed, oh, three or four blocks from us. When we went back, we went that way and saw that it had hit a house on one side of the street and went across and hit another one and, of course, spread junk all over the street. The people were already cleaning that all up, and that was only a few hours after it happened!

Travel Day 6:
A Hole on a Hill

The Christmas Eve story is the one that stuck with me and my sisters—when Dad was in a foxhole for six days and nights in the cold of winter watching the Germans down the hill as they planned their attack. It's the story that was told most often and certainly every Christmas. So it was with great apprehension that I approached this day. Like with all of the other European cities that disappointed Dad in their sheer size now forty-eight years later, I wondered what we might hope to find at Malmedy. The quarter mile that Dad crawled into the town on that Christmas Day likely now would be a freeway.

But first up for the day would be more poking around this area of Kerkrade/Spekholzerheide. Now that we had first-hand information from Pierre about the community, we were fresh to absorb more history. And thanks to him, certainly for this day at least, we were less likely to get lost. A good night's sleep, too, was a boost, there in our lavish upgrade at the Toucan. Even the cards we played until late had a restful effect, serving to settle our emotions after the absolutely thrilling day. "Can you believe it?" I kept repeating that next morning. "We found the battlefield, *and* we found Bertha!" We all shook our heads in wonder and grinned. Our spirits definitely were up there.

Before setting out, we were delighted to indulge in the Toucan buffet, a scrumptious fresh assortment to behold. Ever mindful of our mishaps in breakfast planning along the way, we didn't flinch at the cost—a hotel with a restaurant on site seemed worth every penny. Plus, we were in a celebratory mood. And keeping Dad in his morning toast, eggs, and coffee went a long way toward anxiety-free travel. For someone who preached that breakfast is the best meal of the day, he had been a good sport. The three of us agreed, our thrifty budget plan just might need a bump up.

So it was goodbye to the Toucan and off to more unknowns. The 1944 monastery utilized for resting troops, which was so distinct in Dad's memory—near Spekholzerheide, three-story, L-shaped, on a river—sadly now forty-eight years later would remain for us an unknown. We drove close to the area that Pierre suggested. Looking across an open field, the most we could make out was a wooded area by a river, with commercial buildings on the other side. Like giving up in Paris and Reims even though sensing that much more could be learned with a dedicated search, we settled just for finding the vicinity. After all, no one we had asked remembered the details of such a monastery, and the logical assumption was that the building was now gone. Besides, our travel clock was ticking—our plan was to make it to Nuremberg that night.

But oh, for a little more research back then and a little more time. Today I have uncovered at least references to the monastery, or abbey as it was called. *The History of the 120th Infantry Regiment* mentions a monastery for rest near Kerkrade—this is exactly where we were. And, thanks to the Internet today, a Thirtieth Division website includes this comment by an unnamed veteran: ". . . the Roduc abbey in Kerkrade served as a divisional rest area with USO shows, movies, and actual sleeping beds." Dad had it right.

But back to our itinerary: The Margraten Memorial wasn't on it. We weren't even aware of it until our visit with Pierre and Bertha and frankly, our planning might not have included it even if we had been aware. Cemeteries weren't our thing, so we thought. But now feeling an obligation to the Urlings' hospitality, that's where we headed. Anyway, Margraten wasn't far away, only a few miles east of Maastricht, just as Pierre had directed. We agreed that we could stop a minute before heading south to Malmedy and then on to Nuremberg.

Officially known as Netherlands American Cemetery and Memorial, Margraten is Europe's third largest war cemetery for unidentified soldiers who died in World War II. Over 8,000 American soldiers are buried there. The site is sixty-five and a half acres with a Court of Honor, a reflecting pool, and then in precision the thousands of white stately crosses marking graves.

This was the area of the heightened Allied military operations in northwestern Europe from June 6, 1944 to May 7, 1945. The nearby Cologne-Boulogne highway was used by Hitler's troops. But dating back even to the Romans, other historical figures had traveled here too: Caesar, Charlemagne, Charles V., Napoleon, and Kaiser Wilhelm II. Again, we were standing on soil filled with history.

A walk into Margraten naturally instilled an instant somber, reflective mood, like that of any cemetery. But this site of honor commanded more. The giant stone slab behind the statute of a grieving mother says it from the heart of the Dutch people: "Here we and all who shall hereafter live in freedom will be reminded that to these men and their comrades we owe a debt to be paid with grateful remembrance of their sacrifice and with the high resolve that the cause for which they died shall live."

I finally got it—the U. S. flag alongside the Dutch there in Amsterdam where we began and now this memorial site donated by the people of the Netherlands to honor the Americans who served. It was true: the U.S. *had* made a difference in the name of freedom. And this was where Dad fought.

I looked back for him as I walked with Wilt to the car. He was standing at the top of the steps chatting with a stranger, with the memorial a backdrop. I snapped a photo. True to his resourceful nature, he always found time to socialize and learn along the way. But there was more to it—Dad told us in the car that this stranger from Holland deliberately stopped him to say, "Thank you, sir, for your service. Thank you."

We left Margraten with our thoughts to ourselves. For all our searching of details, we had almost lost sight of the sacrificed lives, war's ghastly reality. Dad likely fought alongside some of the men buried here. I noticed as

1992 – Dad visiting with a local at Margraten, Netherlands, American Cemetery. (Author's Collection)

we drove off slowly that Dad watched out the window at attention until we had passed all of the long rows of crosses, like a mental salute.

The mountains, trees, and rivers of the Ardennes offered fresh relief from the densely populated areas we had just covered. And, after the sobering reflection at Margraten, we each welcomed a renewal of sorts from nature. Now on the road to Malmedy, we were back into Belgium and the forests. And now we were in search of that Malmedy hill.

The Germans used the forests to their advantage in concealing armored divisions when they launched a surprise attack on December 16, 1944, in a last-ditch attempt to split the Allied forces. Characterized by dense forest and few good roads, the Ardennes seemed an unlikely location for a German offensive, but this eighty-mile stretch of land is precisely where they planned their attack. Dad's company was suddenly ordered to relocate in response to the attack, and that's how Private Albrecht found himself outside of Malmedy. His foxhole would serve as an outpost to counter an advance on an open hill overlooking stalled German troops below. That was for six days, December 19th to 25th.

As we cautiously made our way into the bustling town, Dad let out a long sigh, the kind of sigh that suggests giving up. "Gosh, this is a lot bigger than I remember. Right about here is where I found the medics, but nothing looks familiar. Nothing at all."

Remember, I had approached this day with great apprehension, and now I had good reason. "But, Dad, remember this is forty-eight years later. Naturally, many of the buildings have been replaced, roads redone. Even *Morgan's* main street is different from forty years ago, right? And Malmedy here . . . was in the war."

"Yah, guess you're right." He rolled his window down as if that might help to recognize the surroundings as we crept along in traffic hoping to spot the hospital, the church, the little bridge, all from 1944.

The best we could do was find the information center, really a gift at this point. And, almost as if to affirm our efforts that this in fact was the place, there at the entrance was an engraved seven-foot stone slab in tribute to the First Army liberation of Malmedy. The understanding young clerk reminded us that the 1944 bomber raids in fact destroyed most of Malmedy. "You bet they did!" Dad piped up, suddenly recalling his story to this unexpected listener. "I was in a foxhole just outside of town when we got the heck bombed out of us for two days from *our own planes*. And when I crawled into town, everything was a real mess, all busted up."

"Yes, sir, you remember the destruction, I'm sure," she nodded. "Well, best of luck on your tour around town. And thank you, sir. Belgium was liberated."

That interaction was more than enough to satisfy Dad—a pleasant person and respect besides. He had accepted the fact that not many young people knew much about World War II any more—those at home anyway—so this encounter took on special meaning.

Regrouped, we got back in the car and headed southeast of town just a mile or so to the Five Points intersection. Our history book had indicated that eighty-six U.S. prisoners had been killed at this location, and this was where we found a memorial of the Malmedy Massacre. From there, we circled the area eyeing hills with open expanses from the surrounding forests. We suspected that the massacre had occurred close to Dad's outpost.

We settled on a hill with enough of the features to reasonably fit the story of the foxhole outpost. In 1944, Dad and his foxhole buddy kept watch below at a house with a wheat stack—now, a farm was at the bottom of the hill along with scattered neighboring houses. We walked the hill and the fence line in the brisk air. So immersed we were in the 1944 scene, we even looked for any small dips in the ground as for a foxhole, now almost five decades later. Standing midway down the hill, Dad finally said, "Yah, this could be it. Looks about right." I was the one to sigh then, but in relief.

We treated ourselves to Belgian waffles before leaving Malmedy and heading to the autobahn. The long drive ahead of us now on our way to Nuremberg would be a perfect time to get out the tape recorder again.

***

December 21-23, 1944: "On the night of December 21-22, the first snow blanketed all of the Ardennes forest. Problems of camouflage and winter equipment arose. Here, too, we were short. But winter also brought clear weather, and beginning December 23 our planes were out in force for the first time since the attack began, with a flight of over 2,000 planes . . ."

The Battle of the Bulge, Robert E. Merriam (Ziff-Davis Publishing Company 1947; Ballantine 1978)

Private Albrecht:
CHRISTMAS IN A FOXHOLE

We weren't going to cross the Roer River until after Christmas. While we were waiting for orders, we fixed up a little church back there a ways from our hole. It had the windows out, and we patched them up and got a little evergreen. We would pick up the foil that our airplanes would drop to knock radar off. We decorated our tree with that, and then the chaplain, he was trying to get something lined up for singing for Christmas.

But then, of course, before Christmas, they came and hauled us up to the Bulge. That was at night, and it was something to wonder about because we were packed so thick in those trucks that if you would have fainted, you wouldn't have fallen an inch—you would have stayed right where you were. We didn't know what was cooking at all.

They said, "Grab your rifle, all the ammunition you can carry, and one blanket and your pack, and come on!"

Out in the truck we got, and they said, "If German planes come over and drop flares, we'll stop the trucks and everybody get out and run to both sides of the road. Get off of the road so they don't nail everybody."

Well, we hadn't gone so very far, and then a German plane came and dropped some flares. You couldn't move in that truck—we were so packed in. They would have to open that back end—you know, these were just stakes, not enclosed trucks or nothing—and there we were standing with doggone rifles and couldn't get out. Why, heck, by the time you'd ever all get out of that truck, those planes would have been gone home already!

Evidently the planes didn't spot the convoy. If they did, they didn't do anything about it. Then we went on. They said, "Now if we get stopped again, don't even try and get out of the truck because you can't anyway. Just have your rifle and put it up, and when the plane comes over the top of you, everybody pull the trigger and just let a bunch go. Maybe we will be lucky enough to hit one. But don't try to get out."

Well, then we made it up into the Bulge, and we still didn't know what the score was . . . that our lines had been broken up there, the American lines.

We stopped in the Ardennes. There was a house there, and a lady and a man were in there. They were Belgian. There was a lot of snow. Our officers went in there, and they come back out and said, "All right, you guys come on in."

Their barns are part of the house too—all in one. You can go from the house right into the barn without going outside. They said, "There's a hay barn up there. Get up there right away and lay in the hay—nobody smoke—and probably get a few winks of sleep."

So we did, and the officers stayed in the kitchen down there with the old man and the old lady. Finally they got us out again and loaded up. We went up a little farther, and then they didn't know where in the heck the enemy was.

From then on we walked. We got up to Malmedy, and came walking in over the bridge coming into town. We got up to this one end, and then the sergeant and I were given a telephone and wire to pull, and they said, "Go out on that hill, on the slope of the hill by the fence, and dig a hole—you are an outpost. You listen to Germans down below ya."

We were in that hole for six days with no overcoat and no overshoes—we each had only one blanket. When one blanket got wet, we let it freeze and put it over the end of the foxhole so one of us could sit under there and not have the snow fall on him. It snowed every day until two days before Christmas. We watched night and day—off an hour, on an hour, twenty-four hours a day. Our canteen froze, so we licked snow. We had some little cans of cheese that we'd nibble on.

Our hole was behind this fence with the green stuff on it that looked like evergreen, but it was a weed. We'd peek through it and watch the Germans down there in the house right below us and listen to them, hear them talk. A lady was the boss—she was givin' orders. We'd call back and let our headquarters know what the Germans were doing down there.

The Germans had a bunch of tanks and halftracks—not that we could see all of them, but we knew they were there. There was like a wheat stack down there. You'd see half a dozen Germans come out of the house, walk over to that haystack, and you didn't see them any more. They evidently had an opening there and then a tunnel from there to someplace.

Then on the twenty-third, the Germans evidently decided it would be a good time to counterattack. That's the reason we were out on that bare hill because there were no trees right there, and if the Germans were going to come up with tanks, that's where they'd have to come up. Otherwise they'd have to use the highways, and they knew those would be mined. It would be no use trying that.

They came up the hill during the night, probably about 1:30. We heard this tank start up, and we listened—you could tell they were coming closer. We couldn't see them. It was too dark. They got closer and closer and finally, why, the lead tank—it was a big one too—he was just about up to us.

We were lying in the hole, and I had the phone and was hollering for artillery. I said, "Shell number nine. Shell number nine, and hurry up!!"

The artillery would draw a map, and they would make squares and number them, and I knew our number was nine where we were. Well, then they called back quick and said, "Say, we can't shell number nine. That's where you are!"

I said, "That's where they are too—just let 'er come and get going!!"

Boy, they started putting artillery in there—I'll tell you, it was comin'! All we had to do was lie there and hope we didn't get a direct hit. Then the lead tank decided that wasn't the best idea to go up that hill, so he turned around with the rest of them, and they went back down the hill. We would call in and tell them to keep lengthening the artillery fire another one hundred yards farther, or so, just by sound. When the shell would explode, we'd get a little glimpse of where they were. Then in the morning when it got light, we saw that one tank and one halftrack were knocked out!

On Christmas Eve—of course, I'm saying Christmas Eve, but we didn't know it was Christmas Eve, we had no idea what day it was or anything else— we had, you know, two days of bombing already from our own planes, and we were black from the dust from that and everything else. There was always shooting going on and sirens blaring in the distance from nearby towns. With all that going on, we were half frozen and couldn't feel our legs.

Then, all of a sudden, pretty close to midnight everything got quiet, just as quiet as could be, and there weren't any shells going off, no sirens sounding. I looked up, and one star was so doggone bright, you wouldn't believe it. You'd have to go through it—but it just shown like . . . oh, I tell ya . . . and I told the sergeant, "Look up there. Look at that star!" Of course, you remember we didn't think it was Christmas. That was farthest from our minds. "Look at that star! Man, oh, man, I never have seen one like that!" I believed the war had ended because everything was so quiet. We were just kind of stumped.

Then the buzzer buzzed on the phone, "Hey, you guys down there, there's somebody going to come down to the hole so don't get trigger happy!" We looked up. We could see a little movement up the hill. Some guy—he evidently had a white outfit on—he lay in the snow, and it was just like he swam down the hill to us. Pretty soon he got to us, and he just got up to our hole. He had two socks, one for each of us. He said, "Merry Christmas, fellows. I'm goin' to get the hell out of here!" He turned right around and started crawling back up through the snow to get up in the bushes again.

We looked and said, "Well, my gosh, this is Christmas Eve!" We never realized it. You know right then that real bright star just brought something to my noodle—I thought somebody was saying, "Hey, I haven't forgotten you yet. Don't worry about that. I'm still watching." That's just what it seemed like . . . something special done that.

We opened the sock, and the mate was in there. That didn't mean nothing—we didn't change socks anyway and never had nothing off. But, there were seven candy bars in each of our socks. The first bar we took out was an O'Henry. I'll never forget that. Of course, you realize that this was the fifth day we were out there with not much of anything to eat. So the sergeant said, "Okay, Albrecht, here's what we'll do. Let's peel the paper back on our O'Henry, and we'll eat half of it. Then roll it up, put it back in our sock, and then tomorrow we'll eat the other half. Then that way we'll have enough candy here for fourteen days, because there are seven bars. We don't know how long we're going to be here."

Well, that sounded pretty good. "Okay." So we peeled the wrapper off and then we ate . . . and neither of us said one single word until we had all seven candy bars eaten! You couldn't quit! It just tasted so gol darned good that I don't even know what all the bars were, but it didn't make any difference. All seven were gone, and all that was left was a bunch of wrappers.

Then the next day was Christmas Day, and that was the day I crawled into Malmedy. I had called on the phone and asked if there was any way to get some aspirin for the pain in my chest—I couldn't stand even a teaspoon in my pocket, it felt like it was too heavy against my chest. They called back and said,

"You have permission but you don't have to do it. If you want to get on your hands and knees and crawl into Malmedy"—which was probably a quarter or a half mile, a pretty good distance. *"You have our permission because there are some doctors there. You can get something from them."*

Well, then about noon on Christmas Day, that's when I decided to go into town. I just kind of lay flat in the snow and sneaked along staying behind whatever I could. I got in there and saw some smoke coming out of a house, and I went over there. Some tankers and TDs had plugged up the windows, and they had a stove going in there. I got some hot water and made a cup of coffee, some powdered stuff. I wrote a note to Lorraine and the girls and told them to mail it. They told me that down about three or four houses some doctors had moved in.

I went down there, went in, and the doc came out of the dining room. He had a turkey leg in his hand he was chewin' on. That's as far as the Christmas dinners got. He stuck a thermometer in my mouth and so forth. I sat there and he went back in to chew down some more turkey, and then he came back in and looked and kind of frowned—he got some more equipment, started testing and pretty soon he told the guys, "You get a stretcher for this guy." They got one and I had to lay on there and they pinned a tag on my jacket: "Bronchitis, Pleurisy, and Pneumonia." They wouldn't let me even get up from the stretcher, let alone go back to the hole like I was going to.

I later learned when I asked some of our fellows about my buddy in the hole that the next day he got a direct hit and was killed.

***

December 15, 1944: "A private airplane, carrying American jazz musician and band leader Glenn Miller, disappears in heavy fog over the English Channel while flying to Paris. No trace of the plane, crew or passengers is ever found."

1944 Newspapers, www.historic-newspapers.co.uk

Private Albrecht:
PARIS GENERAL

After the doctors told me I had bronchitis, pleurisy, and pneumonia, they lifted my stretcher on a Jeep—on the back end just across. They had taken a bulldozer and made a path through town. The hospital was on the other side of town, and these guys were supposed to take me there. We got just about in the middle of the town, and our P38s came over with 500-pound bombs and started lettin' us have it again. We made it across—stuff flying all over—but none of us got hurt on that deal.

They got me over to the hospital. It was so full from our own planes bombing us three days. The Belgians were getting killed by the dozens. It was just one of those mistakes.

They had just room enough to slide me in the hallway, the last one before the door. I wasn't in there very long. They gave me something, I guess to go to sleep. Anyway before I did go to sleep, why this Belgian lady came in. She was a young lady, a blonde, and she had her little girl in her arms. Both of them were bloody from head to foot—one arm was off the little girl and one leg, and I think she was dead. But the mother was hollering for help. I fell off to sleep and then pretty soon I was gettin' loaded in an ambulance giving us a ride up through the Ardennes over to Liege, Belgium, a train center where a hospital train was waiting for wounded guys.

That night when we got over to Liege, they stopped and opened the door. That's when I woke up, and I looked out and here was a whole bunch of Germans standing there talking German. I thought, "Holy cow! Here we got captured in the hills!" Then pretty soon here comes an American sergeant hollering at them guys to get hold of the stretchers and carry them in.

They had the tent set up out there in the pasture. Now the reason they didn't have it right in town—there was a hospital in town—was I guess because the town was catchin' it. The Germans were aiming buzz bombs at Liege. That was a big rail center, and they wanted to knock out the rail deal so that we couldn't use it. So this tent was set up there out in the field, and they had some beds there, quite high, just on the grass, and I got laid on one of them.

A nurse came by and gave me some pills to take and said, "When the buzz bomb comes over and the motor stops, just flop off, fall on the ground." The tent was full of holes already. There was one buzz bomb every five minutes—we timed it. The motors would quit and then "whoom" and the old tent would shake. I don't know, we were probably in that tent a couple of hours.

Then they took us down by the train station and put us in the railroad cars. That took several hours before they ever got that full—stretchers one on top of the other, right on the walls of the cars, with things out there where they would set you right on. I think they were probably about three feet high in the car and then as long as the cars were—they were all stretchers. I remember that the guy underneath me was a pilot. He'd got shot down, and he had one leg broken and an arm broken, and they had him in casts. His other foot was cold. I had a sock on and told the nurse, "Take that off and put it on him." She did. That made him feel better.

All that while these shells would come in and just shake the train. You'd think, "Oh-oh, boy, the next one better not be a direct or that'll be it . . ." Then finally, why, the old train whistled and we started going, and boy was that a wonderful feeling—heading for Paris.

I don't know how long a trip it was to Paris—you lose track of time, all of a sudden you doze off from stuff they give you. We finally got there and they took us in ambulances to the big General Hospital, right uptown. They said, "You'll be in here no more than ten days. At ten days, if you're good enough, you go back to the Front. If you're not good enough, you go to another hospital."

I think the second day we were in there that's when the Glenn Miller Band was there to play. Of course, Glenn wasn't there—they were expecting him. Some nurses got a bunch of wheelchairs and they took about fifty of us down into a small auditorium. There was his band all set up, and I think the drummer was leading it. He said that any minute Glenn probably would show up. He said they lost track of his plane, and they figured he probably had to land where there wasn't communications, and so they were waiting for him. But then they played for us for two solid hours, all the pieces, which was really good. Glenn never was found.

We were in that hospital ten days. You had a chart on the end of your bed like any hospital. When the doctors would come to mine, they said, "Nope, not yet."

Then the ambulance came and loaded a bunch of us up and took us to what used to be a girls' school in Paris, not right uptown, out a little ways, but in town. I think it was a three-story building—there were no elevators, just those round stairways going up to the different floors. We were on the third floor. Those poor devils had to carry us up there on those stretchers. They were catching heck from the officers because they were tilting us. We were the first patients in there. All the doctors and nurses and ward boys and all that were there. They had just come over so that was all new to them. We were in there, oh, a good three weeks. Up in our bunch, I think we were all pneumonia patients from the Bulge.

Our day-nurse was Betty Correll—she was from Superior, Wisconsin. The night nurse, we called her Pepilinsky—I don't know where in the heck she was from, but she was a real good scout. Well both of them were.

The second day we were there the Red Cross gal came up and wanted to know what she could do for any of us—if we had any shopping we wanted done, buy some Chanel No. 5 for us to send home to our families, or whatever. She wanted to know if anybody had any relatives over there. We had one kid from New York City. He was an Armenian, and, of course, he had never been overseas before and never seen his aunt and uncle or cousins or anything, but he knew they were in Paris. He just knew their last name so he told the Red Cross girl that. She never said any more but the next morning the whole family was up in our room— mother and dad and the daughter and a son. The son was a coiffure, a hairdresser, and I don't know what the gal did. But anyway, one of that family visited our room every day while we were there. If they would bring something—I remember one day they brought some strawberry jam—that was enough for the eight of us or sixteen of us, whatever was in the ward. They brought that up and the kid understood a little bit of Armenian from his folks, of course, but otherwise he couldn't really talk it or anything, but we got along good with the guy.

The one that was a hairdresser, after he was there a couple of times why some of the guys said to this kid, "Hey, when your cousin comes up here, why don't you see if he can't get some good cognac and bring it to us?"

"Well, ya, I can get the kind you guys buy, but," he said, "the good stuff that probably would take a couple of weeks. You probably won't be here."

We decided and said, "You go ahead and try. If we are still here, we will get it—if we are not, well then it's too bad."

Well, one day this hairdresser came up. He was carrying a briefcase, got up in the room—no nurse around—and out he comes with that quart of stuff and put it under the kid's pillow. After he left that night, when Pepilinsky came in, then he brought that bottle out.

We had about four or five inches of snow on the ground in Paris, and we were up three floors and no elevator, just those winding stairs. We had all been in bed all that while and got nipping on that quart and cleaned that up. Of course, being in that shape, why, it didn't take much and you could feel that in a hurry. We got up out of bed and just with pajamas on and slippers we went down those flights of stairs with the nurse and walked out. There was a vacant block, and then right across there was a French theater. We all walked over to that theater and went in. Of course it was all French—you couldn't understand anything—and so we got the heck out of there, and we came back to the hospital and went up to our room. There wasn't a one of us that had any ill effects from walking in that snow and everything else out there! But Peplinksky—some of the higher-ups caught her feeling pretty good, and she caught particular heck.

It was quite a time. A little later on when we had a pretty good appetite, they'd come by with this kind of a wagon deal with all the trays on from room to room. When they'd be taking stuff into a room across the hall, some of our guys would be sneaking out grabbing a tray or two and shoving it under our beds so we'd have some after we had our regular meal.

We were in there probably another week, and then they took us out and sent us down to near Le Havre. They had what they called a hospital for the final recuperation. I always remember when they hauled me in there and put me in the bed, I went to sleep and in the morning, why all of a sudden here comes the doctors and everybody jumped out of bed and bent over and they all got a shot in the butt. I thought, well what in the heck, and of course I didn't get up and when they came by I said, "What's cookin'?"

"Oh," he said, "they all got venereal disease in here."

"What the heck am I in here for?"

"You won't be in here long—they'll be getting you out of here. We didn't have any other room."

I was stuck in there for that night, and then a little while later I got in a different building with guys more in my shape. I was there, oh, about a week or a few days anyway. It was still winter—cold—and, oh, boy, if you just stuck your head out and you didn't have your cap on or helmet, why you would catch it from the doctors, "Oh, you got to watch out—you had that pneumonia, now!"

Pretty soon we were released, and then you went to the train station and got in these forty-by-eight boxcars. That's a boxcar that holds eight horses or forty men—that's the way they were lined up—big cracks in the floor—and we stayed in there all the way back up to the Front again. They would stop for something to eat once in a while. We got up in Belgium and they'd stop and had a train station with a kind of kitchen. They had a big thing full of mess gear, and you would get out and grab one of them and go through the line and get something to eat and then get back in the train and keep on going.

We stopped for dinner or something, whatever it was, and I got through the line and got up to the window where they served you giving you whatever it was, meat or potatoes or something—and here our old medic from my squad was behind there with a big spoon. He was putting potatoes on the mess gear, and I looked and said, "Doc!"

He looked, "Oh, for heaven's sake, Albrecht!" And boy, off come his apron and he come out around the side, and he and I went over to a table. He was a full-blooded Jew. He had a Jewish name—I don't remember it—big tall, lanky guy—swell guy, boy, I tell you. You couldn't beat him.

He always said that they couldn't hit him. Whenever we were being attacked and somebody would be down, he went right out no matter what was flying. Shells could be coming, and that didn't bother him a bit. He would walk out there and bend down and start taking care of his guy out there. He was catching it from the officers. They said, "Doc, you're too important. Don't go out there until it eases up!"

He wouldn't listen. If somebody dropped, why he was out there. He said, "They can't get me anyway." But then he said, "Well, I found out they can." A bullet came in—a sniper lady shot our lieutenant, and he was such a heck of a nice fellow. Boy, Doc went right out there to get him. There was a big rock there, and he got down by the lieutenant and saw he was dead, got it through the head. Just then the sniper shot again and it glanced off the rock and went through our doc's ear, right through the side. So he had that all bandaged up.

Then, of course, I had to leave. Well, then every time we would get to a place where we would eat, there were some doctors. I had orders when I left the first place that every time you stopped, you had to report to these doctors. So we were getting up into Belgium, and we stopped and I got out and went into the docs. They kind of checked me out, and that was our last stop before we went up to our division, up to our troops.

I don't remember what city, but we were kind of in a château outside of town where we stayed. Then the next day a truck came and was going to take the guys up to the Thirtieth. Of course, I was one of them, but the doc wouldn't let me go. He said, "No, I'm keeping you back here. Tomorrow you and I are going in the Jeep. We're going into Liege, Belgium." He said, "The hospital is pretty decent there, and I want to get some x-rays."

So the next day, he and I went into Liege, and he took some x-rays and finally he said, "Well, that takes care of it. Now you can go back to your unit. I thought you probably had a touch of TB starting. If you would've—if I could have found any indication of it—I would have sent you right home."

About that time, I wasn't so sure I wouldn't have minded having a touch of TB. But I didn't, so I went back to the Front.

You have to always go to a dentist, too, when you get released. I went to the dentist. "Well," he said, "you will be going back now but that's going to be over before you ever get back to the Front."

But he was badly mistaken. I got back in time to start gettin' with the crew to cross the Rhine River.

Travel Day 7:
Two Soldiers

THE REASON WE VEERED OFF our tight course in the Belgium/Netherlands/ Germany area to visit Nuremberg wasn't because that was another area where Dad fought—he was there *after* the war ended. A laundry unit was his assignment for several months until he had orders to go home. But laundry duty didn't guarantee enemy-free duty just yet. The fragile nature of war hostilities can pose ongoing threats to safety. So it was that Dad liked to tell the story of the laundry unit. And so it was that we headed south into Germany knowing that the last day or two we would be back in his favorite Netherlands before our return flight.

Our drive the previous day from Malmedy brought us to our overnight in Wurzburg, just short of Nuremberg. Travel lessons thus far were sinking in so we knew that venturing into the thick of Nuremberg late in the day would likely lead to trouble in finding accommodations. Besides, a nicely appointed older hotel presented itself at just the right turn in the road, and at a legitimate time for happy hour. Good food, drinks, and cards put the finishing touches on a big day. Also noted again in my journal: "down comforters."

Leaving Wurzburg, we chose a southern approach to Nuremberg, which took us through the fascinating city of Rothenburg ob der Tauber. Here again, through no particular planning on our own, we were treated to a destination for tourists from around the world—a medieval walled city. The fanciful streets of the city are noted enough to have been featured in many movies. Thankfully for historians, nearing the end of the war, wise decisions by commanders on both sides spared the city from total destruction. A city with this rich story certainly deserved more of our attention but again we needed to remain faithful to our mission. I wondered how many more of these European travel hotspots we might be storing up for another time. After a brief stop to experience the streets, we waved goodbye to Rothenberg ob der Tauber and continued on our way.

Had we known, however, the difficulty we would face the next few hours just down the road in Nuremberg, we might have changed our itinerary. City travel can have that effect. But, had we changed our plans, we would have missed the astonishing find of our trip. That find came as really a sideline in our search, like a prop on a set.

For several hours we had been maneuvering traffic in this dense European Metropolitan Area of Nuremberg, as it is called, to encompass surrounding Nuremberg communities. Going this way, then that, then back again, we asked for help from bystanders, policemen, and gas stations (recall "attendant guy"). Finally, we landed at a museum where, thankfully, we didn't let go of those helpful people until we had some answers. My journal says "sort of successful."

The suburb that Dad recalled he pronounced as "Berfahnbach," but no one we asked knew that name. Dad's memory always has been a wonderment to anyone who has known him, but maybe this time he heard it wrong, spelled it wrong, pronounced it wrong, or just plain misunderstood. But, with more description, the patient and thorough museum clerks were able to piece together the details and point us on our way. It was the 1945 U.S. air base near a creek which Dad vividly recalled that seemed to make sense to them. The Furth area of Nuremberg was where we headed.

We pulled up to a park-like area along the Regnitz River. The cool, sunny day was perfect for a stroll in nature, and that's exactly what we did. Whether or not this was the exact location didn't matter at this point when we could be free of the car. We knew at least that we had made a good effort. Dad agreed. So we reviewed our long string of facts, and Dad gauged the surroundings with his 1945 memories. "Yah," he said, "this could be it. That laundry unit was just a couple of big trailers anyway, so they wouldn't be here. And the building we stayed in probably was torn down. But the air base, well, I suppose it could be over there." He pointed across the river.

We must have looked confused and particularly foreign because a stranger approached us. "Can I help you find something?" he said in broken English. When we first arrived at this park area, I couldn't help but notice the man smoking a cigarette, standing with his bicycle. He had white hair and looked to be in his sixties, and most impressive, he was dressed in a suit and tie—a gentleman on a bicycle.

I'm sure we looked dumbfounded, out of the blue like that, and not expecting to hear English. But Dad was quick to answer. "Well, I sure hope you can, sir. I was here at the end of World War II with the U.S. Army, and this here is my daughter and my son-in-law. We're trying to track down where I was stationed. Berfahnbach was the place, on a creek like this, and with an air base."

"Yes, the air base was just across the river there," the man pointed where we had been looking. "See that open area?" He smiled. "I think you found it."

That exchange began a unique friendship. George Forder knew about the war too but as a *German* soldier. He was only nineteen years old serving in the German navy in the North Sea when he was taken prisoner. What were the chances we would just *happen* to run into a German soldier from the war? We all gasped at the coincidence of our crossed paths. Well, the bond between the two veterans was immediate—two soldiers, same war, different sides, here at this park forty-eight years later sharing their lives. Wilt and I could only look on in wonderment.

And then it got even better. George invited us to his home, which was only a few blocks away. We followed in the car as he aptly maneuvered the traffic on his bicycle obviously a matter of routine, so distinguished he looked in that suit and tie. His home had the same quality of care as his attire, certainly well-established, a two-story stucco with a view to the river. We nervously stepped inside. That's when George told us that his wife didn't live there any longer—he had been caring for her some thirty years at a nursing home. But he brushed that sad story aside as he briskly grabbed a bottle of wine from the wine rack. "Today we must celebrate!" he announced. "This is my finest wine!"

The photo of Dad and George toasting has a warm glow with the sun coming into the balcony, the amber wine in their glasses, and their smiles. When duty called, these men had served, but today they were celebrating long life and friendship. Wounds do heal. Dad's take on the war comes to mind: If country leaders were the ones on the front lines of battle, wars would stop.

What could I say? The high emotions of this travel day would stay with us. They buoyed us even through that afternoon when we were challenged with the dark reality of the Nazi movement. But that search I'll mention later. This day belongs to the laundry unit . . . which led us to George.

1992 – A toast of newfound friends, former enemy soldiers, George Forder and Russel Albrecht. (Author's Collection)

***

February 11, 1945: The "Big Three"—Franklin Roosevelt, Winston Churchill, and Joseph Stalin—meet in Yalta to discuss war strategy and post-war issues.

www.militaryhistory.about.com

Private Albrecht:
CROSSING THE RHINE

It was sometime at the end of January 1945 when I got back from the hospital and we were taken to a little town close to the Rhine River. We were taken in there at night. We were stuck in a couple of big houses, and they said, "Don't come out, don't roam around the outside because Germans are living around here, quite a few of them. You don't want them to see you because even these people, they could report that to their headquarters."

We got in those houses, and they had sand tables in there that showed us the Rhine River—in other words, where we would cross—it showed after you got across. There would be a railroad track up there. You would see that. You would see four or five rail cars on that track and one of them tipped—they emptied them *sideways—and that's where you would regroup after you got across. You got that secure, that's where you regroup—and we'd see where we were to go from there.*

"Okay," we figured. "Well, I suppose we're right by that site."

We stayed there two nights and two days, I believe. Then the trucks came and took us just like that in the night—I suppose 12:00 or somewhere in there—and then we went quite a ways.

Well, you see the idea of the Army was they knew the people there would watch us and knew we were in those houses and that's the area where we were going to cross. There was no doubt. So they would notify their headquarters, and they would have troops waiting for us. Then, of course, at night we would get in these trucks and then we would go down the river a heck of a ways before we finally came to the spot where we wanted to cross. That was to throw the Germans off.

We got down there, and there was a big dike. There was a big field ahead of the dike. We lay down there and dug a little hole, not deep, maybe a foot, just so you were protected. They said, "Wait until we call."

We lay there about an hour or something like that in the field. Then they gave the order, "Come on, get across the dike, and there will be boats there waiting."

The engineers had like a rowboat. Only seven guys would get in there and then the engineer who ran the motor. We'd get in there—everybody on one knee and one up holding your rifle so when you hit the other shore, they'd hit it fairly fast so that you just flew out of there, but you were in a position that you could take right off.

They had machine guns on the right and the left, off quite a ways, shooting tracer bullets across the river. Of course, at night you can see them going by. That was our area, in between those

1945 – "View from the levee on the west bank of the Rhine." (History of the 120th Infantry Regiment)

two machine guns. That's where we'd do the crossing. They said, "Now don't go beyond those where that fire is going because then you're in the enemy territory completely."

We got, oh, halfway across the Rhine. The boats had fifty or fifty-five, I forget which, horsepower Johnson motors on, and ours quit! And, of course, it was a pretty good current!

We started goin' down, down, down, and all of a sudden we were underneath those bullets flying over, and in the meantime, it was just steady artillery fire. Probably the biggest Fourth of July deal you'd ever seen—it just lit up the sky and your clothes were shakin' like you were in a real strong wind, just from concussions.

Well the old engineer, he was really working his butt off to get that motor going again, and all of a sudden, it clicked! We went through the danger zone by probably a block already or something like that, but he scooted right back up where we belonged and got us over.

Well, then we regrouped by this tipped over railroad car, and then our objective was to cut the autobahn, the big highway—to stop the Germans from using that.

***

1946: "We must never forget that we may also find meaning in life even when confronted with a hopeless situation, when facing a fate that cannot be changed. For what then matters is to bear witness to the uniquely human potential at its best, which is to transform a personal tragedy into a triumph, to turn one's predicament into a human achievement."

Viktor E. Frankle, *Man's Search for Meaning*, First published in Austria in 1946 under the title *Ein Psycholos erlebt das Konzentrationslager* (Simon& Schuster, 1984)

Private Albrecht:
THE CELLAR

From the Rhine to the autobahn was a pretty good jaunt. It was late at night. That's when we came up to this prisoner of war camp. We were walking down a tar road in the woods and pretty soon we came up to the camp. A concentration camp is what it was, but the German officers had all skipped out of there. The gates were open and they were gone.

Our guys stopped the whole caboodle on the highway and then the captain, or whoever was in charge, told me and the sergeant—he gave us one flashlight—and says, "Go over and check those buildings."

We walked over, and I'd give the sergeant fire protection while he ran in one, and then he'd watch when I would come over to him and would give me protection. We went from building to building, and they were empty. The buildings had just slats in there for people to sleep on, like bunks, and the slats weren't close together—they were far apart, no hay or nothing else. That was it. Just terrible looking—some windows out which, I suppose, was from artillery fire.

We were going through one building and there was another door leading off. The sergeant was outside the building ready to go for the next one. I hollered at him, "Hey, wait a minute—come on back here!"

There was a door. I opened the door, and I could hear something down there. There were steps going down, but there was a wall on both sides, and at the bottom was a doorway that went into the basement. Well, we started down the steps, and you had to hold your rifles up because of the closeness in there. And it didn't smell too good.

We got down in there, and just that quick, we got grabbed! It was just full of prisoners. They were from all different countries. They had been in there for twelve to thirteen years. Their clothes were all tattered and torn, they hardly had anything on. There were even little babies. There was nothing to eat. Filthy.

We had to break loose and put the rifle on them to keep them back. They were hollering, "Americans! Americans!" They were so glad to see us.

We told them that we were going to leave and they could come up and they could go outside—nobody was going to stop them—they'd be free. They just kind of stared at us like, "What the heck are you talking about?"

What little stuff the sergeant and I had in our pockets, we gave them.

Then we went up and met our troops out on the road. We found a big pit, probably fifteen feet square or something like that. It was full to the top and looked a little crusty. Here it was that when you died or you got a little too sick, you got stripped of your clothes and tossed in there and then another shovel full of lime on you and that would eat you up. It was full of bodies—that whole thing.

Faye Berger with Russel Albrecht

***

1945: "Decca label releases 'Back Home For Keeps,' by Carmen Lombardo, Performed by Guy Lombardo & His Royal Canadians."

Syracuse University Library, www.library.syr.edu

Private Albrecht:
SLEEP WHEN YOU CAN

After leaving the concentration camp on our way to the autobahn, our guys decided there were only a couple hours before daylight so we would stay there until morning. We had been up like two nights and two days and we hadn't slept. They said, "Probably you can get an hour's sleep. You guys find yourselves a hole"—the Germans had a lot of holes there—"and one sleep an hour and then you wake up and let the other guy sleep an hour."

A guy I had with me said, "You go and sleep first."

Well, okay. These holes we were in were right by a road too and then a big forest on the other side. I looked around—it was practically morning and there was a kind of dew and chilly as the dickens. I didn't know where to lay to try and snooze. There was a big pile of cement slabs, I don't know, probably about eight feet square or something like that. I don't know what they were used for. They had like two by twos in between them to leave air spaces. A big pile of them, I suppose ten feet high. I thought, "Well, by golly, it's going to be dry on top of there." So I crawled up there, and I lay down on top of that cement.

I must have just went out like a light—just fell to sleep so quick. Pretty soon my buddy was hollering around there wondering where in the heck I was. I woke up, and here he was looking for me. I came climbing down. "Man," he said, "you weren't up there during the counterattack, were ya?"

"Counterattack? *When the heck was the counterattack?"*

"Oh, man," he says, "did the shells come in!"

I never heard even one! When I went to sleep, boy, I was sleeping.

Then I went in the hole, and he found a spot to lie down. The next day we started out again.

***

1940-1945: "Ancel Keys is a major scientist of our times . . . Keys founded the Laboratory of Physiological Hygiene at the University of Minnesota in 1940 . . . Commissioned by the Government in World War II to study human performance during nutritional deficiency states, he developed the emergency K-ration that was used extensively by U.S. military troops in the war and afterward."   "Ancel Keys," by Henry Blackburn, M.D., University of Minnesota School of Public Health, www.sph.umn.edu

"While the K-rats were designed for only a few days' use under assault conditions, the demands of war meant that soldiers often ate them for days or weeks on end, and boredom and complaints naturally ensued."

"U.S. Army Field Rations," www.usarmymodels.com

Private Albrecht:
EGGS AND COFFEE

I went into Maastricht, and we weren't supposed to buy any food or anything like that. I mean that was illegal. But I was going down the street, and I saw a sign sticking out like a big soup kettle and that's what they called it, "Soup Kettle." That was about two o'clock in the afternoon or something like that, and I thought, "Well what the heck, I'm going in there to see if I can't get an egg or something."

I went in there and sat in a booth, and a young kid came. There was nobody else in there, and he came over and said I should get out because the MPs would see it and I shouldn't be in there. I asked him if his dad was around.

"Ya."

Well he went to the kitchen, and pretty soon the old man came out and came over to the booth. "Ya," he said, "MPs are out there."

I showed him, I don't know, a bar of soap or toothpaste or something out of my pocket and, oh, boy, he gave the kid the key and he went up and locked the front door, and then he gave the kid some money and he went out the back door and came back with two eggs. The old man fried them and brought them out to the booth with some black bread and a cup of coffee. And then he sat in the booth with me while I ate. He asked me how I liked the coffee, and I said, "Good, good, ya!"

"Well," he said, "that's made from ground up dried tulip bulbs!" And that's exactly what it was, but by gosh, it didn't taste bad. I was hungry as heck for it anyway, so maybe that's the reason.

Travel Day 8:
Winding Back on the Rhine

NOW WE HAD A FACE FOR THE ENEMY: George Forder. Might the image of this encounter be a catharsis for all vets? Enemies toasting? Considering their parallel journeys long ago—the nineteen-year-old German boy and the thirty-four-year-old U.S. husband and father, both answering their country's call to service, and now this journey forty-eight years later that would bring them together—one almost certainly has to assume divine intervention. At least that's what I choose to believe. So it was that we had George Forder in mind for the remainder of our trip as someone whose path we were meant to cross.

The Center Nazi Party Rally Grounds is where we headed next, which seems oddly counterproductive in a big way to the high we had just experienced with George. But for the sake of our history hunt, we had this on our list. Dad had visited the site, but most of his stay in Nuremburg was limited to that laundry unit in Furth. Still, we were drawn.

But the names we used when we asked for directions were "Hitler's Stadium" or "Hitler's Arena." Those only got blank shrugs. When someone did direct us to a stadium, it was the new, grand stadium recently built. Finally, it took a passerby with fluent English to understand our question. We weren't far off the path, but no one had related to the name of Hitler.

When we did step into the vast arena, we immediately understood—worn and run down now, this place, for all practical purposes, had been forgotten. The stigma of its past was apparent in its cold emptiness. Weeds were sprouting on the concrete walkways and the stadium seats. No one stopped us from walking the site; in fact, we apparently were the only ones there that late afternoon. Contrast that with thousands of soldiers marching before the *furor* in the very spot where we were standing. I could almost hear the strident chop of their goose step. The grand chamber halls were locked, seeming to hold in the grisly history. Oddly, a helicopter was maneuvering over the field.

Years after our visit, we learned from another visitor to the center that in fact it remains in this state of disrepair as a reminder of the crimes and those dark days of World War II. Germany leaves a cold history lesson in stone and concrete.

1992 – I am with Dad at the deserted and neglected Center Nazi Party Rally Grounds. (Author's Collection)

For us, the sobering reflection now at this late hour in the day sent us hastily back on the road in search of accommodations, drinks, and a comforting meal. Rather than risk getting lost again, we headed out of town and were relieved to land a second night at picturesque Wurzburg. The warm memory of George was back on our minds, and we raised our glasses a second time. Good is always stronger than evil, I reminded myself. That day we became acquainted with both.

Now, to catch up with my journal, for this new day, we were ready to head north to the Aachen area again. First on the agenda though were the sights at Wurzburg, which we missed in our hurry on our way south. Like a theme for the day, at breakfast we were treated to the German/Austrian culture when we eyed a local in his jaunty *lederhosen* drink a tall stein of beer to accompany his eggs and cold cuts. Differences, we agreed as we stifled our giggles, can be refreshing.

Again, this city of Wurzburg, dating back even to the Bronze Age, deserved a full history lesson. The stark fact that the city was ninety percent destroyed in March 1945 can easily be lost in the amazingly accurate replication of the historical buildings. And the fact that those who rebuilt the city immediately after the end of the war were mostly women brings to mind the astounding industry and wherewithal that surfaces in times of war. The Wurzburg men were either dead or had been taken prisoner. In the U.S., when the men were off at war, it was the women who rose to manufacture the ammo and supplies.

We soaked in all we could for the morning and in keeping with the history lesson chose a longer route back to soak in more. The two hundred-mile stretch between Wurzburg and the Austrian border is the Romantic Road, as it is known—picturesque countryside dotted with medieval villages, Baroque palaces, castles, and vineyards. Beyond every turn in the road is a photo opportunity.

But the road also meanders with Germany's Rhine River, a significant demarcation in the war as a natural defense for Germany in the Allies's push eastward. Finally in March of 1945 the Allies were successful in crossing the Rhine at four points and then continuing their assault further into Germany. Dad was part of that effort. Like an espionage thriller, his recollection describes the carefully planned crossing complete with troops moving at night into position, tracer bullets marking the specific river area, and a turned boxcar on the other side for regrouping. This is the Rhine we gazed at now, camera in hand. "Gosh, can hardly believe I did some of that stuff," Dad thought out loud. Wilt and I couldn't have agreed more.

After some gift buying at Boppard, we chose a faster route to the Aakon area. Travel experts surely would wag their fingers for this one—hurrying through a destination popular enough to earn the title "Romantic Road." But the day was wearing on, and the three of us were exhausted. We could not soak in even one more drop of history.

Maastricht, Holland, in that Aakon area is where we found a comfortable older hotel, nicely renovated, and absolutely out of our price range. No matter. A tavern in walking distance served a delicious meal—absolutely out of our price range. It seems that our adventures required celebration.

Finding Foxholes

***

April 20, 1945: ". . . Hitler celebrated his fifty-sixth birthday deep underground in Berlin; he even ventured with a few friends into the gardens of his Reich Chancellery, from which he could hear the boom of the Russian guns. On the same day the American Seventh Army took Nuremberg . . ."

The Pictorial History of the World War II Years, Edward Jablonski (Doubleday, 1977)

Private Albrecht:
COAL SMOKE

When I was coming back from, I suppose Osfeld, we came through Cologne, and we were going to stay there overnight—must have been just a truck with a bunch of guys on, not necessarily all from our Division. We found an old building there to crawl into for the night. It was cold. I don't think it was freezing, but it probably wasn't too far from it. Anyway, we found this old building, and we went in. The whole bottom floor of it was full of GIs who were going to lie around in there someplace for the night. They said, "You got to go upstairs."

Well, the stairway was so wobbly when you walked on it—the building was hit real bad in the first place—it felt like the whole thing was going to cave in, but we went up it anyway—pretty long steps. We got up on the next floor, and then we found a room. Of course, the windows were all knocked out and everything, and the big window had a transom in it. We put some blankets or something over the main windows to block off the cold, and then we went outside and we found an old copper wash boiler and some hard coal. We put that up in the room and found four candle sticks in the building there, and we set the wash boiler on that—I don't know what the heck we put on the bottom but we built a fire on there. Got nice red hot coals, and the transom was open so the smoke could go out there.

It was warming up a little then, and we were all going to go to sleep all lying on the floor. I told the guys, "If you get cold, don't somebody go and close up that dang transom"—because the coal wasn't smoking any more, it was just red hot.

"No, no, we won't close it."

I don't know . . . I woke up and holy smokes, I felt bad, you know, real bad. I wondered, what the heck? The first thing I did, I looked up and somebody had got cold and put the blanket over the transom so we had all that coal gas in there! That's what it was!

110

I woke everybody up. Where I was it seemed the draft hit just right so I think I got the biggest share of it. I went down them steps, probably about 5:00 in the morning, just one at a time . . . sitting. I would lower myself, step by step. I felt sicker than Sam Hill. Then I got down to the outside of the steps, and I just sat there. Oh, about 7:00 some guys came by, and I asked them about a place to go or how I could get something for this, but they didn't know anything.

Finally I started feeling better, getting that good fresh air. Then eventually, why, I was all right. To this day I can't stand the smell of coal gas, when you are burning coal.

1944 – "Briefing today for the flight tomorrow." (History of the 120th Infantry Regiment)

Finding Foxholes

***

1944-1945: June Wandrey of the Army Nurse Corps describes her ward: ". . . such young soldiers . . . nineteen yeas old . . . They're so patient and they never complain. I won't be able to write . . . often and here are the reasons why:
> *Bed 6, penetrating wound of the left flank, penetrating wound face, fractured mandible, penetrating wound left forearm.
> *Bed 5, amputation right leg, penetrating wound left leg, lacerating wound of chest, lacerating wound right hand.
> *Bed 4, massive penetrating wound of abdomen. Expired."

The Greatest Generation, Tom Brokaw (Random House, 1998)

Private Albrecht:
WOUNDED AT THE AUTOBAHN

We were gettin' up right near the autobahn. I think we were probably not over two blocks from the autobahn when some shells came in, and a chunk of shrapnel got me in the shoulder. That took care of me, and I had to go back.

The medic fixed it up and cut the sleeve off of the jacket and shirt, put a sling on it, and then I got back to where they had a weasel—like a Jeep, only it has tracks on it.

Two young fellows who were brand new to combat duty were driving the weasel. I got on it—of course, four were on stretchers, and I was sitting because I didn't have to lie down.

These guys started out, and I didn't like the way they were going. I said, "Doggone it, you aren't going the right way!"

They just looked, you know, like, "Hey, what the Sam Hill's the matter with you? We know what we're doing." They as good as told me that. "We know what we're doing. Don't worry about us."

"Well," I said, "I'm worried a little bit more than just about you. You're gettin' into enemy stuff here!"

"No, no, no, we know the way."

You could see they were wrong because the road we were on was covered with dust from all these shells, and there wasn't a track on it. So you knew we weren't using that. But they went. You couldn't tell them anything.

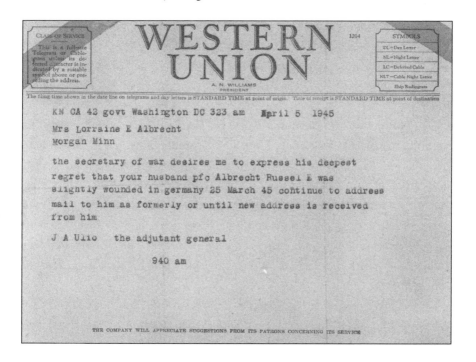

Then we came to a corner where they had to turn, and a shell had hit right in the middle of that corner and made a pretty good hole. There was a little clearing right there. When we went in there, the weasel kind of tipped sideways when we made the corner. Then the guy up on the top stretcher fell off and fell down in the road. He didn't know it because he was out anyway.

So we quick stopped and got out—I jumped out then too. I had one good arm so I could help them get that guy back on the stretcher and get him up there.

We had just got him on the stretcher, and then we started getting shelled from right there in that woods. Some Heinies were in there and started blasting. They knocked the windshield off, and we were down kind of behind the vehicle. I got a chunk that knocked me in the knuckles, not anything bad, just slid by and cut 'em open.

They shot about seven or eight times, and then they had to put in powder bags—that's something you learn in Basic. Then you have a little hush or time in there between shots. So when I heard that many shells, I said, "Come on, get that guy up and let's get the heck out of here!"

So we did—we got him up. We got down the road a little bit, and we had a couple more shells blow behind us. They were still shooting at us, but we made it.

I think those young guys learned a heck of a good lesson there because they thought they knew all about it, and boy, they were so wrong—they wouldn't listen.

Then I went to the hospital and got fixed up there. I don't know what hospital, somewhere in Belgium, I am sure. The main thing was I couldn't have something in that arm—holding my rifle for instance—it was my right arm—and just all of a sudden whatever I had there would just drop, I had no feeling. When I got hit in the shoulder, it didn't dig in much but it cut some muscles or nerves, and every so often that would go limp and whatever I was carrying dropped down to the ground. Then the doctor made a little better sling, and then I didn't carry with that arm at all. When we were going somewhere, I had the rifle in the other hand.

I don't remember how long I was in the hospital, but I don't think over one and a half weeks. Then I was back with the bunch again.

***

May 7, 1945: Headlines in *The New York Times*—"The war in Europe is ended! Surrender is unconditional; V-E will be proclaimed today . . .

Associated Press correspondent Edward Kennedy "reported a full day ahead of the competition that Germans had surrendered unconditionally at a former schoolhouse in Reims, France. For this, he was publicly rebuked by the AP and fired. British Prime Minister Winston Churchill and President Harry Truman had agreed to suppress news of the capitulation for a day to allow Russian dictator Josef Stalin to stage a second surrender ceremony in Berlin . . . Sixty-seven years later, the AP's top executive is apologizing for the way the company treated Kennedy."

Minneapolis Star Tribune, May 4, 2012

Private Albrecht:

OUT OF THE INFANTRY—END OF THE WAR

After getting out of the hospital in Belgium, when I got back on the truck to go back to our outfit, they were up by Magdeburg, forty miles from Berlin. Nobody was doing anything. There was the river there, the Elbe River, and everybody wondered why in the Sam Hill we weren't going across and going into Berlin. The officers said that we didn't have enough supplies up that far because while I was in the hospital, the troops just went right lickety split on up there. There wasn't hardly any resistance. In fact, the Germans would rather we come in than leave the Russians get in there.

So after I got up there, then my records came up and they called me in the building there and said, "Say, with your age and since you've been hit twice, that's enough infantry for you."

So I got stuck on a truck with another guy and sent back into Belgium. I know we just got, oh, maybe five or ten miles out of Magdeburg, and we were sitting in an open truck—just those slats up there—and all of a sudden a sniper let a couple bullets come and they hit those boards by us, but that's all. We didn't see where in the heck he was. Well, when your troops move fast like that, then there are a lot of snipers left back in there that don't want to give up. Just like the Japs did over on the islands. They'd bypass some, and here they'd still be out there fighting their heads off. So we had a sniper try to pick us off but he didn't do very good.

115

So we got back into Belgium, and we weren't there too long and then the dang war ended. Then I was out of the infantry because they sent me back, that was it—I was out of the Thirtieth Division.

We stayed in an old wool factory there. I don't remember if it was Viviers, Belgium, or Tongres, but it was a very, very long little city right in a valley. I don't think it was over two blocks wide any place, mostly just length. They had a street-car running the whole distance. Well, we celebrated then uptown. We weren't supposed to go down there, but we did. The Belgians, they were having beer and hard boiled eggs and stuff, and they were celebrating so we got in on it.

Travel Day 9:
Solemn Fast Food Fix

A SIMPLE TASTE OF HOME CAN be a powerful force. That was the only defense Private Albrecht had when he broke the rules in search of a fried egg in Maastricht, Holland. Now forty-eight years later, his vivid memory about that simple meal is what focused us on our next search. The sign "Soup Kettle" is what he hoped to spot. Really? Wilt and I didn't have the heart to dampen his hopes, but the possibility that this tiny establishment still existed, not to mention our finding it, was remote to say the least. Nothing! *Niets!* *Nichts!* "Crown Jewel of the South," as it is affectionately known in the Netherlands, Maastricht now is a vibrant city of 120,000 residents.

But Wilt and I could almost envision the 1944 Maastricht that Dad remembered. Situated in that wedge of land next to Belgium and Germany, Maastricht was at the center of conflict. In May 1940, the city was taken by the Germans, but it was the first Dutch city to be liberated by Allied forces—that was on September 14, 1944. Dad arrived in that area soon after. One might picture a hungry soldier sidetracked on one of the quiet streets when he notices a tempting Soup Kettle sign.

But quiet streets were not part of the day now as we ventured out of the hotel La Roi. Maastricht, known for its picturesque squares, its historic inner city revitalized for shopping, and its cafes, pubs, and restaurants, was abuzz. The owner of the Soup Kettle never in his wildest dreams would have envisioned this Maastricht described in the tour books for its "culinary delights" and "cosmopolitan food." Not the fried eggs, brown bread, and coffee made of tulip bulbs that he served.

I could tell that Dad kept his eyes peeled for that Soup Kettle, but we gently shifted our focus to shopping, just to keep in step with the crowds, we said. We found our way to the inner city or "Old Town" as it was called, and there we walked the open-air shops. Not ones to shop just to shop, we were happy to search for items on Dad's list, now that he actually had made it to Europe: Holland seeds, of course, and, slightly out of the ordinary, bike tires to fit his European bicycle back home. We found both items.

The day was windy, cold and drizzly, so we scooted along in and out of shops always hoping to find a warm spot. We came to appreciate the concept of central heat as we knew it back home. We understood now after several days of this chill-to-the-bone feeling, why Europeans wore quality, woolen clothes, layered, and sturdy shoes.

Stopping to visit a vast, stone cathedral with the famous "Madonna" only added to our chill. After a coffee and pastry, we were back in the warmth of the car and, on the recommendation of a tour guide, headed to the Overloon War Museum. The museum is on the site of the Battle of Overloon, a tank and infantry battle during September and October 1944. Again, this was the vicinity where Dad would have been fighting. The towns that Dad mentioned in his stories—Maastricht, Aachen, Eupen, Liege, Tongeren—all are part of what is called the Meuse-Rhine Euroregion. This was the heart of his action until the Battle of the Bulge. So we definitely were on track.

The museum displayed a large collection of military vehicles and equipment in fascinating detail, but its other collection depicted the Nazi invasion with heart wrenching Jewish stories and memorabilia. Neither of the exhibits offered much English translation. We began to drag, and the chilly rain seemingly on cue added to the mood. As we shuffled to the car, Dad finally spoke up. "I didn't see much about the U.S., did you? Gee, I'm getting hungry."

Much as we tried to convince ourselves otherwise, the day had been a struggle. If not for the unrealistic expectation of the Soup Kettle, we might have slapped a high five and celebrated a day of touring and shopping in beautiful Maastricht. Certainly, Wilt and I would not have planned a visit to remember the concentration camps and certainly not late on a dark, rainy day. So much for expectations and last-minute planning.

But an interesting high spot did occur as we found the highway to Den Bosch where we were headed to find accommodations for the night. Out from the depths of a depressing afternoon, lo and behold, the Soup Kettle did appear. Well, it wasn't the 1944 Soup Kettle, but it did have a beckoning sign. This soup kettle, tucked into an historical building just off the square, had unmistakable golden arches. Dad was the one who spotted it. "Hey, look over there. Isn't that a McDonald's?"

So it was. We relished in the home comfort of a burger and fries.

***

April 12, 1945: CBS Bulletin reports Franklin D. Roosevelt is dead.

1945 Radio News, http://archive.org

Private Albrecht:
LAUNDRY INTRIGUE

From the town in Belgium, I got put on a truck and hauled down to Nuremberg with another guy, which was a good long stretch. They left us off at a building, and I said, "Yah, now what?"

"Somebody will pick you up here, maybe in the morning."

Well, we kind of found a place to crawl in one of the buildings there, and in the morning a truck came by and stopped for us and took us out to Berfahnbach, that's a suburb of Nuremberg. I got put in this laundry unit. I don't know if the other guy did or not. I imagine so, but I didn't even get too much acquainted with him.

Anyway, I got in that laundry unit. We had two big trailers. There was a creek right there, and we had trailers pulled up to the creek. Each trailer was a complete laundry unit. It had its own power supply and had a washer and a dryer and a spin

1945 – Dad noted on the back of the photo: "Another view of the main part of Nuremberg." (Author's Collection)

deal, and they'd wash clothes for different units in the Army that needed it—they all needed it. We were there, I don't know just how long, but it was very interesting.

This big building across the creek was where we stayed with a little bridge going across. There was a little shack down there by that little bridge, and there was a water hydrant there also. A gal lived in that little shack—a real good looking chick, dressed good and painted up and a good build. Boy, she was nice looking girl and, of course, the guys all were eyeing her up.

My buddy that I just got acquainted with there went out to guard on that little bridge. Every night they posted a guard on there—why I don't know—the war was over but they still had to watch it, so they'd post one. Well, he was out there, and in the morning he was all excited because that gal came out to get some water out of that hydrant and she asked him to come down and open it up to get some water. There was a wrench on there. He says to her, "Open the darn thing yourself."

She got mad and she called him an SOB and said that she'd killed seven GIs. She told him, "I'll kill you!"

Of course, that got him all nervous. Then in the morning he was telling me about that. "Well," I said, "What'd you do?"

"What'd I do? Well, what should I do?"

"Well," I said, "you had a carbine, didn't you?"

"Yah, but we didn't have any ammunition!" He said, "Even if I would have, what should I do?"

I said, "Well, there better not be anybody—man or woman—that's going to threaten me if I got a gun in my hand. I'll guarantee you that because I'm going home when this thing is all done. I don't want anyone to spoil that now!"

"Oh, golly." He didn't know about that . . .

Then the next day my name was up on the blackboard for guard duty. The guys came and told me about it. "Oh, ya," I said, "well that's fine but there'll be one little difference. I'm not going on the bridge with an empty carbine, I'll guarantee you that!"

"Oh, no, no, they won't give you shells." Of course, none of them had been in any combat whatsoever. They were a laundry unit that came over from the States, and they had no combat experience.

So then I walked down the hallway, and they said, "Where you going?"

"Well, is the captain down there?"

"Ya, but you can't go in there. You got to go to the sergeant first, and then he'll check and see if you can get in to see the captain."

Well, that isn't the way I do it, so I walked down to go in the captain's quarters, and then the sergeant happened to open the door. "Whoop, wait a minute fella," he said. "Where you headin'?"

"I want to see the captain. I just want to talk to him," and I opened the door.

The sergeant said, "I'm sorry, sir . . ." and I walked right in.

The captain looked at me and said, "Oh, you're our new man, aren't you?"

"Ya, ya," I said, "I just got here."

"Oh, ya . . . Albrecht?"

"Ya, that's right."

"Well, what can I do for you?"

"No complaints, that's for sure, but I got to go on guard tonight."

"Well," he said, "you know we got to pass that out amongst the fellows."

"No, no," I said, "I'm not complaining, but my buddy was down there last night, and he had his carbine but no ammunition."

"Well, no, you see the war has ended now, and we don't want any ammunition."

"Well," I said, "I'm sorry, sir, but if I'm on guard, I'm going to have ammunition one way or another. Now that gal down there that lives by the bridge— you know, that good looking one—she threatened my buddy. She said she'd kill him, and she has killed seven GIs already."

There was a lieutenant in there too. They all had a big smile on, and they said, "You mean you would take a shot at that woman?"

I said, "It doesn't make any difference to me who it is as long as they're threatening me—and that's it! I'm going home—I've got a wife and two daughters, and I'm going to go back to them! If I was captain of this outfit, I'd call into Nuremberg and have the military police come out and pick that gal up and get her out of here!"

Well, that didn't seem like it was necessary. They said, "We'll have to see."

So I went out and a couple hours later one of the guys came up. They were all wondering how I was going to fare talking back to the captain—well, actually disobeying an order. This guy says, "What in the world did you say to the captain, Albrecht?"

"Why?"

"Why? Well, you're not on guard duty. They erased your name. They got somebody else on there."

That made me mad because I thought, "They aren't going to take my place. I'm not going to stick that on to somebody else. To heck with it!" So down

121

to the captain's quarters I went again. I barged in there with the sergeant right after me. I was worrying the heck out of him.

"Now what's the matter?"

"Oh," I said, "I see I'm not on the blackboard. How come you took me off?"

"Oh, oh, well, you know we weren't thinking right, you see. You've just come in. You shouldn't be on guard duty that soon. We've got to wait a week or two."

"No," I said, "that isn't the reason. I know it isn't. It's because of that ammunition deal."

"No, no, no. We just didn't think it was time yet for you to be on there."

"Well," I said, "did you take my advice and call the MPs?"

"No, we haven't."

I said, "Well, just remember—that's what I would do if I was in charge of this group here."

Then he gave me a cigar and wanted to know if that would cool me down any. I said, "Well, I sure can use the cigar."

So I went back out. I wasn't going to go on guard—no way—he wouldn't put me back on.

But then that day a military Jeep came in and went up to this little house. Our laundry trailers were just a short ways from them. Two guys in there got out and went up and rapped on the door. She came out, and they talked nicely—you could see that—with her. She got her purse, and they went back and helped her into the Jeep and drove away.

Of course, the guys all had a sort of grin on, you know, thinking, "Well, I suppose Albrecht is satisfied now. They got rid of that good looking chick out there."

It wasn't too long and the Jeep came back and left her off, and the guys went up to the house with her. You could see they were saying they were sorry they had to bother her and so forth. Then the grins got a lot bigger!

Then probably an hour or hour and a half later something like that, why all of a sudden two Jeeps came in there like a bat out of hell—four guys in each Jeep. Boy, they had guns out, and over they went. They kicked the door in, and out she came with handcuffs on! They put her in the old Jeep—not too gentle—and took her into town.

Then everybody had their mouths open. They weren't giggling any more. I didn't find out until several days later that they'd had her in there first and kind *of checked her over. Everything looked fine and okay. Then after they took her back, they started looking up records a little better and here that was a woman they were after. She was the daughter of the leader of the Hitler Youth Movement, and she had killed seven GIs, and they were looking for her! That's when they came back and really clobbered her and got her!*

So from then on, I had no problem with anybody around there. If I wanted to do something, it was fine.

***

August 14, 1945: President Truman announces that Japan has surrendered unconditionally, ending World War II. The formal surrender took place aboard the *U.S.S. Missouri* in Tokyo Bay on September 2, 1945.   www.history.com

Private Albrecht:

CAMP CHICAGO

I'm not sure how long I was at Nuremberg at the laundry outfit, but I know we left Nuremberg and got down by Reims, France, in Camp Chicago about July second or something like that, 1945.

Camp Chicago was right out of Reims, I don't know how far, but it seems it was close. It was a big camp for all kinds of U.S. troops from different outfits. While you were there, they checked to see how many points you had and so forth. If you had enough points, they would take you out of whatever you were in and put you in that outfit to get you ready to go home.

It was a real big camp with a big outdoor theater called The Playhouse, and it was a nice camp. We saw a lot of shows—Nat King Cole, he was on the stage—and this gal, I can't think of her name, she was a very prominent actress, she had broken her leg shortly before she was due to come over and they thought that would stop her, but it didn't. She came with the cast on and crutches.

We had pretty good eats there, American cooks. Of course, it was all dehydrated stuff, but they knew how to fix it. It was the same kind of a deal pretty near every day—you ate and didn't have to get in formation or a doggone thing. We were just waiting to go home, waiting for your transportation. You had your Red Cross tents and so forth. You would go into town all the time and roam

1945 – Camp Chicago—Dad's notes on the back of the photo: "Our big theater, just before completion." (Author's Collection)

around and come back. You had to check in when you came back, otherwise, you could go and eat. If you didn't want to eat, you didn't have to go—that was up to you. I don't think I missed any meals. I was there probably better than two months, something like that.

You could get passes to go into Paris. We went in there a couple of times and into Reims, but, of course, we'd just walk into there. For Paris, a truck, like a bus, would take us in and pick us up at a certain place. There's where I met some guys— this Wagner from Pennsylvania, he was a heck of a nice guy. He had worked with the Pennsylvania Conservation Department and knew a lot about the wild stuff.

Wagner and I would go out in the woods and look for wild boar, and then he showed me the good chestnuts to eat. You know, around home why if you do find a chestnut tree, it's a horse chestnut and they're no good to eat. But these were the good ones. We had on fatigues—we would fill our pockets full of them and come back into camp. We had cement floors and wood sides about three feet high all the way around and then tent over the rest of it. We had a potbellied stove in there, and we would lay those chestnuts on there and when the chestnuts would kind of pop and turn over, then they were done. You peeled them and ate them- boy, they were dog-gone good! You could eat them raw too, but I liked them roasted like that.

That's where I decided to send a box of chestnuts home to Lorraine. I packaged up a bunch of them and went into the captain to get it censored.

"What you got in there?"

"I got chestnuts in there."

"Oh, you got some squirrels at home or something?" They were all laughing in there.

"No, I haven't got any squirrels at home, but these are good eating."

Well, they okayed them. Evidently he hadn't ever tried chestnuts but some of his helpers had, and the next morning I got called back over there. One of them said, "Say, those chestnuts that you sent, could you get me a few?"

You had to kind of think in a hurry because, you see, we always walked out into the woods, so I said, "Well, they are a little hard to find, and it's quite a walk. I suppose if a fellow had a vehicle or something, you know it would be a lot easier. But I'll talk to my buddy, and we can always see."

I went back, and the next day one of the Sergeants came in and said, "Hey Albrecht, any time you and your buddy want to go out and get some of those chestnuts, I'm the Jeep driver. I am supposed to pick you guys up and take you out."

"Well," I said, "that's fine." So then we got him to get a carbine because we didn't have any then ourselves, and we got the Jeep and went out. We were mostly looking for wild pig that we wanted to get—found their tracks but never could get one. But we picked up a few chestnuts and brought them back so we had some for the Captain.

One day while I was at Camp Chicago, I walked into Reims and was going down the street when all of a sudden I heard the breaks squeal, and somebody said, "Albrecht!"

Man, I looked around and thought, "What the heck?"

A guy pulled over to the curb, and I went over there and here was my first guy that I had in the foxhole— Albee! Boy, we couldn't believe it—here he spotted me walking down the doggone sidewalk!

1945 – Camp Chicago—Dad's notes on the back of the photo: Richard, Marcatta, and myself. (Author's Collection)

I was heading for kind of a USO building or something like that. He said, "You go in there, and I'll be right back. I got to take the Jeep back."

He left for a little bit, and boy he was back there in nothin' flat! We really had a gab fest. Here that day when he got hit and got hauled away on the stretcher, why he was in the hospital for quite awhile. When he got the okay, they didn't put him back in the infantry but he was a Jeep driver. He drove the Jeep for Donald Dayton from Minneapolis Dayton's—Donald Dayton was a captain. Albee was from south of Chicago. He was so surprised to see me—that I'd made it, you know, all the way through!

They would kind of bunch you up according to the points you had. If you were married, you got ten points, if you were wounded, you got ten points, and that kind of stuff. I'd never paid much attention to the getting wounded part. I

1945 – Camp Chicago—Dad's notes on the back of the photo: "About seven miles from camp, picking chestnuts. I'm cussing Wagner because it was taking him so long to snap the picture. Notice my pants pockets are full of chestnuts."(Author's Collection)

had the purple heart—of course, I was wounded even before I got the purple heart, but they never had my name or a doggone thing for that time. Of course, that was my own fault, but that would been ten more points. Then I started looking around and asked one of the officers about it. He said, "Well, if any of your old officers are around and they swear to it that you were wounded, why sure."

Well, we checked and, of course, most of them were dead, but there was one and he remembered that very much. So I got that second one and then they gave me ten more points so I could get in a little earlier bracket to head for home.

I finally got out of there and got stuck in another little camp right next to Reims called Camp Vineyard. That was real close to the town. That was for guys with more points. We stayed there just about a week.

***

"The poppy signifies the symbol of war and the renewal of life." *World Book, Inc. Worldbook.com*

Private Albrecht:
RINGS FROM BURRS

While I was in Camp Chicago, I was always looking for things to do—there was a German airplane that our bunch had shot down right there, so I took some burrs off of the motor. One I still wear today. Then I cut a French coin and made two little rings out of a couple of brass nuts that I got off of that motor—for Mary Jane and Diane. I filed them down and got them nice and smooth, and they looked just like gold, and I sent them home.

But I guess the girls didn't have them too long. They were wearing them and Diane lost hers outside by the garden. We had a couple of lots with tall weeds next to us. She cried and cried and cried, and Mary Jane finally felt sorry for her and took

hers and threw it so that Diane would quit crying'. They never did find them again, so I don't know where they are.

1945 – Dad's notes on the back of the photo: Here's some more wrecked German planes. This is the one that I got the stuff to make the girls' rings from." (Author's Collection)

1945 – Russ's notes on the back of the photo: "This is Wagner standing beside a Thunderbolt. This is the kind of plane that supported us at the front. The plane weighs seven tons as it stands." (Author's Collection)

Travel Day 10:
Winds

O UR LAST DAY. IN RETROSPECT, a visit to the ocean again was fitting. Imagine the soldiers looking out to sea as they boarded a ship again, but this time it was home they were headed. For Private Albrecht, that was at Le Havre in France, not far from Omaha Beach where he first set foot fifteen months earlier. And here we were, the three of us road-trip tourists, now having circled back to the Netherlands for our flight home in the morning. The ocean seemed to beckon us for one last look at the beach and pounding waves, promising a bit of serenity from our regimented cross-country travel.

We set off from Den Bosch, "the forest" as it is translated. Liberated by the British in October 1944, Den Bosch had been the site of a Nazi concentration camp, one of the few German complexes in western Europe located outside of Germany and Austria. We might have opted for staying put this last day, off the highways with little risk of getting lost again, just leisurely taking in the various historic sites, many of which remained intact through the war. But the sea was calling us.

1992 – Windmills at Kinderkijk. (Author's Collection)

On our way to the coast, we scheduled a special stop at the village of Kinderdijk, an area where we would see the famous authentic windmills, the Dutch icon known throughout the world. Then too, there would be the tulips we still hoped to see. Even the cold wind and heavy rain didn't seem to dampen our spirits for this one last day of touring.

The Kinderdijk vicinity is most unusual: By all accounts it should be flooded, situated as it is up to seven meters *below* sea level. But the Dutch have an innovative and intricate system to prevent flooding that involves canals and a unique collection of seventeen windmills dating back to the 1700s. This unusual lay of land and water can be unnerving—one can stand looking in the distance and see above the grass landscape only the top of a passing boat which is tucked in a canal. Amazed and enlightened, we inched along the roads to view all of the lovely windmills. In this setting of golden grasses, green patches with grazing sheep, and an occasional resident hunkered down on a bicycle in the brisk wind, even the heavy gray skies lent a beautiful take on our photos.

"Sure is pretty, isn't it? Even the wind . . . it's nice." Dad was in his element. He pulled his cap down and turned up his collar as we stood outside the car for a better look. Now away from the busy highways, the city noise and traffic, the natural world seemed suddenly to appear like a dose of therapy especially formulated for us weary car travelers. Even finally accepting the fact that tulips were not yet in bloom, not even close, we were fully content with the beauty of the Dutch countryside mid-March.

"Nothing like the great outdoors, right, Russ?" Wilt could see that driving on further to see the ocean was going to be a good choice for this last day. "Let's go take a look at the North Sea. Remember, that's where George was stationed."

Good thing we had the rejuvenating windmills because getting to the coast meant getting through The Hague. Our experience of being lost yet again gave new meaning to the city's name: The Hague translates roughly to "the hedge" or "the wood." Countless wrong turns thrown in with unfortunate detours sent our blood pressure back up to borderline high. That is, Wilt and I were feeling it. We had agreed that this, our last day of our once-in-a-lifetime trip for Dad, needed to be special. For once, just once, we needed to know our way around. Instead, this thicket of a city had us foiled again. As we took turns darting to VVVs for tourist information, Dad waited patiently in the car whistling that nondescript tune he whistles when he waits.

It's no wonder we lost our way in this city of a million people. Though Amsterdam is the capital of Holland, The Hague is the administrative capital, the seat of government, even including several international courts. The city was the site of the world's first peace conference held in 1899 and is known today as "the City of Peace and Justice." Situated just inland from the North Sea, the city also is called "the Residence" because many of the members of the Dutch Royal Family reside in the chic neighborhoods. And despite the formal tones of government at work, the city also boasts lively night clubs, eateries, and shopping, along with its museums and cultural attractions.

Of course, the chic neighborhoods and lively entertainment were not what we were after, but the sea. Just get us to the sea! At long last, after more than a reasonable number of stops, and around that last bend, there it was—not the upscale seaside resort Scheveningen, touted in The Hague as the best on the Dutch coast, but a simple, plain, seemingly unending, beach. The gushing waves, the raw wind, the big cloudy sky—we took it all in. And like Omaha Beach, we were the only ones there. Our thin jackets were no match for the weather this day so we soon took shelter back in the car, but we sat a long while in silence viewing out the windows, absorbing the powerful seascape.

"I told you about that rough ride home through that end-of-November North Sea storm, didn't I?" Dad's eyes were fixed on the horizon.

1992 – The North Sea. (Author's Collection)

"You sure did, Russ. These waves we're looking at here, are probably calm compared to that, right?" Wilt and I smiled.

"Darn, right," Dad smiled back. "And don't forget, out there someplace is where George was on a German boat for old Adolf. That's about the time I was fighting in the Ardennes, I suppose . . ." He paused. "That dammed war was a big one."

We stayed a while longer until the sun was sitting low in the sky. We felt confident of our return trip because our last helpful VVV clerk had mapped our route cautiously back *around* The Hague. A clear shot to a hotel in Hoofddorp, so we thought.

Hoofddorp, with close proximity to the Amsterdam Holland Airport was a good choice for convenient accommodations, but not without a logistical struggle. Now late in the day, the heavy traffic with the unaccustomed canal crossings involving lift bridges, slowed our progress to a crawl. Dinner again would be late.

But somehow the tighter schedules we aimed for at the start of our trip now had a softer edge, and that seemed okay for Dad. I began to realize that this eighty-two-year-old, small-town, Midwestern guy accustomed to scheduled days, regular meals, and a cup of coffee for only $.25 including refills—also could be an easy-going, fun-loving traveler. Why was I so worried? After all, Russ Albrecht had always been an eager learner, curious, adaptive, clever, judicious, and above all, outgoing and positive. Why should any of that change because of age?

So now nearing eight o'clock as we finally sat down with our beers and his "brandy seven," Dad joked and laughed and rallied in our travel mishaps, as well as our finds. And then he paid us the ultimate compliment: "You two sure put on a nice tour. Yah, couldn't have asked for more. You betcha."

My wish for a perfect trip really did come true.

Just down the street at Panekuken we found our dinner. I wrote in my journal, "Good, but *very* expensive." That seemed appropriate for the occasion.

Faye Berger with Russel Albrecht

***

1944-1945: "In the summer of 1944, the War Department published a pamphlet entitled "Do You Want Your Wife to Work After the War?" Designed as one of a series of GI pamphlets which officers could use to provoke discussions and forums, the pamphlet tried to impress on its readers that women's roles were changing, but the dominant voices were those that spoke against women's working."

No Ordinary Time, Doris Kearns Goodwin (Simon & Schuster, 1994)

Private Albrecht:
NO MAIL

When I went up to the Bulge on December 15th or somethin' like that, they took us up and, of course, no mail. I didn't get mail then. On Christmas Day I went to the hospital and I got into Paris, but they wouldn't let me give the address of the hospital to send home so I could get some mail. So that length of time I didn't have any mail. By the time I got back out of the hospital, my mail hadn't caught up with me yet. It had been making the circuit. See, I was in the hospital in Paris for ten days in the big General Hospital, and then I got moved out to another hospital in Paris and I stayed there, I forget how long. But anyway, no mail. Finally, I tried to write the address of the hospital and they cut it out so when Lorraine got the letters, there was no chance of finding out just where I was. Well, then I went back up to the Front and they said, "Well, your mail will catch up to you." But then I got hit and back to the hospital again. All this while that mail, I guess, was making the rounds but not getting to me. So then I got sent down to Nuremberg and from there to Reims, France.

On the second of July I got 104 letters! On the third I got 102, something like that—it was over 100! All these letters and someone had tied string around them, and Lorraine had been getting her letters back home with string around saying they had no way of finding me. Well, that made her mad, and she contacted the postmaster in Morgan but didn't get a response. Then she called in to the State or wrote in, but nothing there. She kept getting letters back that she had written to me—but she was getting mine right along so she knew I was all right.

The last letter I got from her wasn't the one I should have had. There was one I should have had before, but they didn't always come quite in rotation. The last letter I had she was saying she hoped that Diane would heal up and wouldn't have any ill effects and so forth . . . and I had no idea what in the heck had happened. I figured that she probably ran out in the street and got nicked by a car or something like that! I later learned that Diane rode her tricycle down the steps at our house and landed on her face.

But anyway, that was six months that I didn't hear a word from anybody and then, like I say, on the second of July, I opened up that first 104 and got my Christmas packages, what few was there—they were all moldy, whatever was in them. They'd been in shipment that long. I didn't know where they'd been. I didn't open them all because the guys in my outfit, when they would see packages, they all helped you in a big way! They tore the first one open, and that's one I got from my folks and it had Christmas candy in it. You know the old twist, the old Christmas mix in a cellophane bag—well, that had melted flat, the whole package was flat as a pancake and it looked just like bacon. That red in there made them streaks. The guys said, "Oh, man, you got bacon here!" and they ran to find something to fry it in. Then I got a hold of it. I said, "You don't need to look for something to fry it in—that's just hard candy that melted."

Then Alice Rands, a neighbor from Morgan, sent me a box of fudge, because she knew I liked fudge—and the guys had opened that. By the time I saw what was in there, there was only one piece left for me! They had eaten all of it, and it was so moldy you couldn't tell it was fudge, you know, just covered with mold—but down it all went. They didn't pay much attention to it.

This was in Camp Chicago when I finally got the letters. One day they called me from the tent, and I went up to the Captain's quarters—here was a fellow from the U.S. The Postmaster General of the United States got the letter from Lorraine really chewing him out for not getting my letters that I should have and

so he sent a man over to find out just what the heck caused that so they wouldn't have that happen again to somebody else. I suppose it probably did help.

1944 – Biggest thrill: letters and packages. (History of the 120th Infantry Regiment)

***

Thanksgiving Day 1945: President Truman's Proclamation—"In this year of our victory, absolute and final, over German fascism and Japanese militarism; in this time of peace so long awaited, which we are determined with all the United Nations to make permanent; on this day of our abundance, strength, and achievement; let us give thanks to Almighty Providence for these exceeding blessings. We have won them with the courage and the blood of our soldiers, sailors, and airmen. We have won them by the sweat and ingenuity of our workers, farmers, engineers, and industrialists. We have won them with the devotion of our women and children. We have bought them with the treasure of our rich land. But above all, we have won them because we cherish freedom beyond riches and even more than life itself."　　　　www.presidency.ucsb.edu

Private Albrecht:
GOING HOME

After Camp Vineyard, they sent us to Camp Herbert Tareyton—they had them all named by cigarettes—on the English Channel, down there by Le Havre. We were there a few days before we loaded.

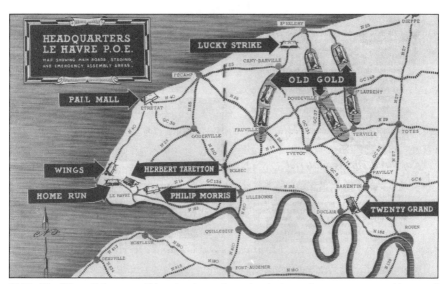

1945 – The "Cigarette" camps—"Map showing main roads, staging and emergency assembly areas," Your staging for the States, Headquarters, Le Havre, Port of Embarkation, Transportation Corps, U.S. Army. (Author's Collection)

Our ship was called the U.S. Wakefield. It was a big ship—held 7,000 of us on there anyway. It was kind of odd when we were going up the gangplank— everybody had to have their sleeve rolled up and you got a flu shot, whether you wanted it or not. They said we were guinea pigs, that it was a flu serum. They were going to see how it was going to work.

Of course, you couldn't have any weapons on you or along with you unless you had your permit for them. I had a permit for a French forty-four revolver and then a bunch of knives. I also had a German flare pistol that I would liked to have taken home, but I didn't have a permit for it. They let you know before you went on that if you had any of that stuff, and if you didn't have a permit, not only would that be taken away but you'd get off the boat and wait for a different one. So of course everybody was throwing that junk in the English Channel there—getting' rid of it if you had more than you should have. We never did get searched. We could have had a whole barracks bag full, and it wouldn't have made much difference.

1945 – Loading the *Wakefield*. (Author's Collection)

We started for home. It was real, real rough in the Channel. The weather was bad and rougher than the dickens. We just got started, and I asked a sailor, "Holy smokes! This is really a rough old sea, isn't it?"

"Oh, man," he said, "you haven't seen anything. You wait about two and a half days and then we'll be right smack in the middle of a good end of November North Sea storm—and you'll know what a storm is like!"

And boy, we sure did—holy mackerel! But for some reason I never had the slightest feeling of gettin' sick. My appetite was big, and everybody was throwing up all over the place. Where we slept I had a top bunk so I wouldn't get thrown up on. The floor was full, the walls were full, the stairway was full. No matter where you looked, somebody had thrown up. All the poor guys were sicker than dogs.

Only seven of us they would let out on the deck, and that's if we had a rope around us. The first railing on the deck was sixty feet above the water and the ship would lay over on its side so that the waves came up on that—so you have an idea. And you'd swear it never was going to straighten up again . . . but it would. We had that, oh, half way across the Atlantic, and then it started to calm down and we got out of that storm. They told us one night that in so many hours then, "We're going to hit the Gulf Stream."

"Well, so what?"

They said, "You'll find out when you get there."

All of a sudden it got quiet and the air got warm and nice. You couldn't believe that you were off that rough stuff, but they also told us that we wouldn't be in it very long. "We'll be going right straight through it—and when we get through it, we'll be back in our rough weather again."

And that's exactly the way it panned out. Now how that works I have no idea but it did. Then a little later, it calmed down, and it was better seas although it was raining when we came into Boston, I remember that.

All of a sudden somebody hollered, "There's the U.S.A.!" and we were all up on board there looking over the edge . . . and there it was! Boy that really looked good, I'll tell you that!

Boston is where we landed. They had a camp right near the docks. It had sort of barracks there, and we went in there, I think just overnight. To start, when we got in, everybody went in the mess hall. By the way—we got in there on Thanksgiving, the end of November, that was Roosevelt's Thanksgiving Day. They had turkey and all the stuff, you know—boy that was good! But of course, a lot of the guys still had that effect from being on the boat, and they still couldn't eat. But I could.

Then we all figured, "Oh, boy, you know, we could get a good haircut now, something in America, and they told us they had a bunch of barbers." They were civilian barbers, not Army barbers. They were in the camp, and they charged their regular fees, whatever it was, but it was high priced—we didn't give a rip. We came in there, and they said, "You want the works?"

"Yup, yup." That meant a shampoo and everything else with a haircut. I guarantee you I went in, and I said, "Ya, I want the works." I had my hair washed and cut and trimmed, all lined up, and dried—at least it was supposed to be—and I betcha it didn't take five minutes! They charged like Sam Hill. You went out of there dripping down your neck, and the hair looked like Sam Hill. Boy, I tell you, those guys made a fortune in there. You get 7,000 guys coming in there and all want their hair washed and, why, holy mackerel, if that wasn't a screwed up mess!

Then in Boston we got on a train—we called it the Milk Train. They stopped about every doggone stop. We went, I think, until Buffalo, New York, and there we crossed and went up into Canada. I remember some of the Canadian towns were like Paris, London, and so forth. And then I don't remember where in the heck we came back down into the States but finally wound up at Camp McCoy, Wisconsin—that's where we were discharged.

At Camp McCoy some fella, a young guy, said his dad who lived in Minneapolis was coming to get him. I got in with him and he wanted to know if I knew the address in Minneapolis—you see, my brother Roy and Dad were going to be down at Uncle Al's to pick me up. We drove and got into Minneapolis, and he drove me right up to their place. I went over to Uncle Al's, and then Roy and Dad, they met me there. It wasn't too long, and then we started for home.

They warned us on the boat when we were coming into the U.S., "When you guys get into Boston now, don't all rush for the phone to call your mother to let her know you're here—unless your mother is young." They had so many that all of a sudden when they landed they'd call their mother, probably you know, older, and say, "Here I am!" and 'boom' they dropped over with a heart attack.

So I didn't do any calling at all. In fact, they even suggested like as soon as you get home, just don't barge right in to your folks. Let them know ahead of time that you're home and you'll probably be there the next day. That's what I did with Mother. Of course, Lorraine—there I went right in—Dad and Roy dropped me off at our house. Then the next day I went over to see Mother.

Note: A final story about Russ's first day back in Morgan wasn't included in the taping session. When asked about it in the fall of 2003, when Russ was ninety-two years old and in failing health, he simply recalled:

"I had the two girls—each had a flag—walking on each side of me, walking downtown."

***

1945: The original Pledge of Allegiance was written by Francis Bellamy in 1862. "No form of the Pledge received official recognition by Congress until June 22, 1942, when the Pledge was formally included in the U.S. Flag Code. The official name of 'The Pledge of Allegiance' was adopted in 1945. The last change in language came on Flag Day, 1954 when Congress passed a law which added the words 'under God' after 'one nation.'"
www.legion.org

Afterword: Stars & Stripes

O NE OF THE BEAUTIES OF A TRIP is the after-effect. Whether it is a beautiful scene that lingers, a bumble that amuses, a new-found friend who connects, or simply an appreciation for differences, we return home for the better. Long after the bags are unpacked and the normalcy of life at home resumes, the things learned enrich even our everyday experiences.

For us, enrichment showed up quickly in the form of letters from George. As an eager new friend, he included photos of himself, his house, his neighborhood, and nearby historical sites, including the birthplace of Henry Kissinger. He sent maps of Nuremberg and specifically of Furth where he penciled in the park where we met and its proximity to the other sites we discussed. He sent a page from a magazine featuring the notable Franken wine that he served us that day on his balcony. And he asked that we visit again when we might spend more time. In his letter dated January 10, 1993, he wrote "I hear, read and I see in the television, that we have and become not the best times in the States, Germany and the world: unemployment, oppression, fire, war, etc. But you and [me] have overcome same hard times and so we will do it in future."

That same year at Christmas, we received a card from Elisabeth Brunck of Nuremberg, who identified herself as George's long-time friend. She gave us the sad news that George had passed away.

The Christmas card exchanges with Bertha and Pierre started up again, and now Wilt and I were in the loop too. But after Dad died in 2003, somehow I let the connection slip. Perhaps I had Mom in mind. Perhaps this next Christmas I will pull out that address again.

After the trip, my interest in the war only intensified. I located an organization dedicated to the Battle of the Bulge veterans, and it was through that avenue I learned of the fiftieth reunion to be held in St. Louis, Missouri, that December 1994. Three phone calls later—one to Dad and one to each of my two sisters—we got busy planning our trip. This was the perfect "sisters with dad" bonding getaway that I had only imagined. The only thing better would have been for my late sister to be with us. And it was at this reunion that one of Dad's stories took on an even more special relevance—the "bright

1994 – Sisters-with-Dad trip to St. Louis for the fiftieth anniversary of the Battle of the Bulge. (Author's Collection)

1998 – I am with sisters Deb and Diane, with Dad, Frances Albee, and his grandson. (Author's Collection)

star" that Christmas Eve in 1944 was acknowledged by the veterans there and even featured in the reunion logo.

Frances Albee, the foxhole buddy most notably linked with the pigeon story, came to visit Dad in 1998. And here's the effect of social media just budding—Frances had asked his grandson to search the Internet for Russ. Then Frances and his grandson drove from rural Illinois for the special visit. The Morgan Messenger wrote, "Russ Albrecht's first foxhole buddy fifty-four years ago visited him recently . . ." WCCO Television even drove to Morgan to cover the event. And again, my sisters and I took the opportunity to honor the occasion: We served a meal of Cornish game hens—granted not pigeons, but close enough.

Frances only lived another year after that visit. He told us that he never had talked much about the war, and when he decided to search for Russ, he did it in private, when his wife was away. Thanks to his grandson, Frances achieved his wish.

Dad lived a good long eleven more years after that trip. His foremost enrichment of course was a good supply of story material for chewing the fat at the pool hall each day. After all, he might be the only U.S. World War II vet with a German vet as a pen pal.

As for the audio-taped stories, well, this is where good karma, or an angel of safe-keeping, or whatever term you prefer, came into play: The tapes were forgotten. Granted, they were transcribed in their rough fashion, but then stored never to surface again for eleven years. There in that drawer mixed with miscellany from other trips and odds and ends in storage, were the tapes, the transcript, the photos, the journal, even the smooth stones from Omaha Beach. That drawer could have been a snapshot of my harried life. It was Dad's failing health that got me back on track: I needed to assemble the stories for our family, and pronto. Frantically, I organized and typed, and frantically Wilt and I sorted and pasted and copied. So it was, that four days before Dad died, Wilt and I presented him with the finished book as a Christmas gift.

From then on, that book of stories has been brought out at our family gatherings, and one of us, usually a grandchild, has the honor of selecting a story and reading it to the group. It's like Grandpa Russ is with us. But the value goes much deeper: While all of us now have a better understanding of the common foot soldier in World War II, the theme of patriotism is carried forward. Our children will fly the flag, then their children- the tribute will carry on.

Dad didn't live to see the World War II Memorial—he died just four months before it opened on April 29, 2004. But I know he was honored each time he spoke to students about his service to this country. Of the many thank you notes he saved, this one especially must have been gratifying and brought a smile: "Thank you, Mr. Albrecht, for sharing your stories. I learned more from you in an hour than I learned in a week of class."

My story wouldn't be complete if it didn't include this one last find. It didn't happen until eighteen years *after* the trip. That's when I was dabbling in writing and found myself researching some of the war stories. Always in

1994 – Above: Russ talking to students. (Author's Collection)

1993 – Russ explaining his medals to students. (Author's Collection)

amazement at the names Dad would spit out, like the memory was just yesterday, it was a fact check that I was doing. Remember Red Degenhardt from the tank explosion? He was on that tank with Dad when it was hit by the blast of a German Tiger Royal hiding in the hedgerow. Well, I honed in on that unusual name, Degenhardt. My search lead me to a list in the back of the *History of the 120th Infantry Regiment* entitled "Killed in Action, Missing in Action, or Died of Wounds." And there I found Red Degenhardt, rather *Hollis* G. Degenhardt. Now very intrigued, I dug further. Thanks, again, to the miracle of the internet, I located an obituary and a memoriam, then a list of possible phone numbers. I called a number, then another, then another . . . and *then* I spoke with Elaine Degenhardt, a sister-in-law, age eighty-seven, living in Independence, Louisiana. "Yes," she replied, "Hollis was his name, but we all called him "Red" because of his red hair. Fun loving and loved to fish, that was Red." His wife had left him so he had no children, and except for Elaine Degenhardt, only nieces and nephews were left in the family.

By now, my heart was racing. I just had one more question: Why was the obituary dated 1946, two years *after* Red's death, with a memoriam ten years later containing these words "wounded somewhere in Europe"?

"His parents died thinking Hollis was still alive," she answered matter-of-factly.

What was I to say? How could I respond to that statement except to give her the facts of Dad's story? For me to be that person informing a family of their soldier's death—in an explosion on a tank outside of Erberich, Germany, on November 22, 1944, and with my father—was chilling.

When I hung up the phone, I became overwhelmed with emotion and cried. We humans *are* connected, I reaffirmed. Sharing our stories is a link.

Need I say, writing this journey has been a journey in itself. Whatever was missed or glazed over in our high-intensity travel, I now have had an opportunity to study and digest—the cities, the landmarks, the battles, the veterans. I'm in awe of that generation. I'm in awe of the soldiers. And my work isn't finished: Nurse Betty Correll from Superior, Wisconsin, who was there with Dad at Paris General is on my list, as well as Private Killinger from Pennsylvania who paid for the doll, Pepsi, the lieutenant, Private Wagner from Camp Chicago, and Private Clarence Dale, who perished like Red Degenhardt on that tank. The journey continues.

Bibliography

Books

Ambrose, Stephen, *Citizen Soldiers*. Simon & Schuster, 1997.

Bonhoeffer, Dietrich, and Wayne Witson Floyd, *The Wisdom and Witness of Dietrich Bonhoeffer*. Fortress, 2000.

Brokaw, Tom, *The Greatest Generation*. Random House, 1998.

Frankl, Victor E., *Man's Search for Meaning*. First published in Austria in 1946 under the title *Ein Psycholog erlebt das Konzentrationslager*. Simon & Schuster, 1984.

Goodwin, Doris Kearns, *No Ordinary Time*. Simon & Schuster, 1994.

Jablonski, Edward, *The Pictorial History of the World War II Years*. Doubleday, 1977.

Merriam, Robert E., *The Battle of the Bulge*. Ballantine, 1978.

Officers of the Regiment, *History of the 120th Infantry Regiment*. Infantry Journal Press, 1947.

Periodicals

Life, "OPA Toyland," November 13, 1944.

Life, Special Issue, A Letter to GIs, "Farms," September 25, 1944.

Minneapolis Star Tribune, AP correspondent Edward Kennedy "reported a full day ahead of the competition . . ." May 4, 2012.

Morgan Messenger, "WWII Foxhole Buddies Reunite After 54 Years," July 22, 1998.

Steckel, Francis, "Morale Problems in Combat," *Army History*, Summer 1994.

Winona Daily News, "Japan Surrenders," August 15, 1945.

World War II, "The Story of G.I. Joe," May/June 2012.

Websites

American Battlefield Monuments Commission, abmc.gov

Archive, "1945 Radio News," archive.org

Blackburn, Henry, M.D., "Ancel Keys," University of Minnesota School of Public Health, sph.umn.edu

City Map HQ, citymaphq.com

Defense Media Network, defensemedianetwork.com

English—The Free Encyclopedia, en.wikipedia.org

Explore the Planet, LonelyPlanet.com

George Washington University, *The Published and Recorded Works of Eleanor Roosevelt*, "My Day," November 16, 1944, gwu.edu

Google Maps, maps.google.com

Historic Newspapers, December 15, 1944, historic-newspapers.co.uk

History, "This Day in History," history.com

History Learning Site, historylearningsite.co.uk

Holland, holland.com

Hurricane Science and Society, hurricanescience.org

Lifetime, life.time.com

Lost Images of World War II, lostimagesofww2.com

Lumey, L.H., Stein, A.D., Kahn, H., van der Pal-de-Bruin, K.M., Blauw, G.J., Zybert, P.A., Susser, E.S., "Cohort Profile: The Dutch Hunger Winter Families Study," *The International Journal of Epidemiology*, 2007, ije.oxfordjournals.org

Maplandia, maplandia.com

MapQuest, mapquest.com

Military History, militaryhistory.about.com

Military History Online, militaryhistoryonline.com

Minnesota Historical Society, "Fort Snelling's Last War," 2009, mnhs.org

National WW2II Museum/New Orleans, nationalww2museum.org

Netherlands Windmill Area, kinderkyk.com

Official Army Operational Unit Diagrams, army.mil.org

Skylighters, skylighters.org

Syracuse University Library, "WWII Songs," library.syr.edu

30th Infantry Division, Old Hickory, oldhickory30th.com

The American Legion, "History of the Pledge of Allegiance," legion.org

Trip Advisor, tripadvisor.com

USO NYC, "History of the USO," usonyc.org

U.S. Army, "U.S. Army Field Rations," usarmymodels.com

U. S. Declarations of War, ibiblio.org

U.S. Department of State, Foreign Relations of the U.S. Conference at Quebec, 1944, digicoll.library/wisc.edu

University of California Santa Barbara, "The American Presidency Project," presidency.ucsb.edu

Veterans History Project, loc.gov/vets

WWII Axis Military History Day-to-Day, feldgrau.com

World Atlas—Atlas of the World is an Educational Resource, worldatlas.com

World Book, Inc., worldbook.com

Acknowledgments

OF COURSE, A SOLDIER'S FIRST-HAND account is a valued, rich piece of history. Thank you, Dad, for leaving that with us. Each of your stories in that famously captivating style of yours always drives home a point—we learn and are inspired, we pass it along. Even in the dark days of war, your positive spirit held on. Thank you for this legacy. Somehow I know that you are here keeping an eye out.

Thank you, Wilt. The inspiration, encouragement, patience, and loving advice—you have been a true partner in this project of love. I am blessed. And your eagerness to help with whatever was required for the task at hand in this book business, well, that partnering is priceless. Your determination to preserve Dad's stories is a worthy example of attending to priorities, getting it done.

Thank you, Diane and Deb, for your total support. As sisters, we have always been drawn to Dad's stories, and we have especially cherished them since he's been gone. His gentle sense of humor, so contagious, I know we each have. And I hope we each have that positive spirit of his, that resilience, to get us through any tough times.

Thank you, family and friends, all of you, for your interest and encouragement in this history project. Diane, your special memories as a little girl gave me a perspective of Mom's life as a young mother with her husband off to war. I can picture her with you and Mary Jane gathering at the dining room table where she read the letters to you. Molly and Mike, you have offered helpful insight from another generation and steadfastly fueled me with the energy I needed. Bella, your creative know-how with videos is downright professional. Diana, your prodding for more of Grandpa's soldier stories has been a motivator. Laura, you shared with me *The One Thing* by Keller and Papasan, which kept me focused when down to the wire. Running friends, you have always been so attentive when I have rattled on as we run the lakes each week. Marcia, I'm still indebted for your advice long ago to read Anne Lamott's *Bird By Bird*. Annie, you put me on to Doris Kearns Goodwin. Lisa, it was at your book club that I got the idea of adding the brief historical perspectives. Susie and Roy, hooking me up with a cool radio show for Memorial Day was a gift. Stan, hosting me on that cool show was a gift. Norma, your generous time in offering me feedback in your own busy author life was beyond expectations and truly appreciated. And Team Libra, for attending to all of the last minute favors I've requested while away from my writing desk, I am so grateful.

Thank you, those who read parts or all and caught the details I missed: Molly, Diane, Jim, Deb, Greg, Karen, Norma, and Wilt.

Thank you, Corinne, at North Star Press. You recognized the importance of my project. Cheers to the regional press!

Thank you, those of you in various military positions who counseled me. And especially, thank you, World War II veterans I've met along the way, for your examples of true grit, whether or not on the battlefield, during that extraordinary time in history. Your service gave us the freedom we have today.

About the Author

Maybe it was the twenty years as a paralegal that prepared Faye best for the pure joy of creative writing. Material too was abundant from years of her dad's vivid storytelling and from her own experiences growing up in small-town America—Morgan, Minnesota.

In 2004, Faye submitted "Russel Albrecht, The Soldier," to The Veterans History Project in Washington, D.C.— stories she compiled from her dad's narration of his experiences in Europe 1944 to 1946. Now, in *Finding Foxholes*, she features those stories in her travelogue/ memoir about a trip when she and her husband drove with her dad across Europe retracing the 1944 route.

Her book in 2010, *Gumption, Lessons on Old Age, Loneliness, and a Hotdish* reveals that same resilient spirit of her dad, but in late life. Based on *Gumption*, Faye now engages groups in lively discussions on the subject of "Positive Aging."

Long distance running is central to Faye's personal "health plan." While in Mexico, she was inspired to write "South of the Border," which was featured in "Cross Culture Running," *Running Times Magazine*, March, 2006.

Faye has a Bachelor of Science degree from the University of Minnesota. She volunteers at Ambassador Good Samaritan Nursing Home in New Hope, Minnesota, and for Medtronic Twin Cities Marathon. She and her husband have four children and seven grandchildren, all in the Twin Cities area. She and her husband reside in Golden Valley, Minnesota, and for three months each year, in Manzanillo, Mexico.

www.fayeberger.com